Growing Stevia for Market

Farm, Garden, and Nursery Cultivation of the
Sweet Herb, Stevia rebaudiana

Jeffrey Goettemoeller

Prairie Oak Publishing
Maryville, Missouri

Growing Stevia for Market is written for informational purposes only. It is not intended to diagnose, treat, cure, prescribe, or prevent any medical condition or replace the advice of a licensed health practitioner or other professionals.

Growing Stevia for Market is not intended to provide all information on the subject matter covered. While every effort has been made to assure the accuracy of this book, there may be mistakes in content and typography. The author and publisher assume no responsibility or liability with respect to any alleged or real damage caused, directly or indirectly, by information contained in this book. Inclusion of company names, contact information, web sites, product names, and other resources do not represent endorsements by the author or publisher. If you do not want to be bound by this disclaimer, you may return this book to the publisher for a full refund.

Copyright © 2010 by Jeffrey Goettemoeller
All Rights Reserved

ISBN 978-0-9786293-5-9

Library of Congress Control Number: 2010932098
Library of Congress Subject Headings:
Stevia
Herb Farming
Herbs—Marketing

Cover and interior photos by Jeffrey Goettemoeller unless otherwise noted.

1.0

Prairie Oak Publishing
221 South Saunders St.
Maryville MO 64468
www.PrairieOakPublishing.com
www.GrowingStevia.com

Contents

List of Figures – vi

Acknowledgements – viii

Preface – ix

Introduction – 1

1. **Climate and Day Length** – 7

   Plant Hardiness Zones – 7
   Perennial or Annual Production – 8
   Choosing a Stevia Field Production Cycle – 11
   Perennial Production with Winter Dormancy – 11
   Photoperiod and Leaf Yield – 15
   Sunshine and Glycoside Content – 16
   Stevia's Critical Day Length for Blossoming – 17
   Determining Day Length – 19
   Field Transplant Timing Above 15° Latitude – 21
   Field Harvest Timing Above 15° Latitude – 24
   Field Transplant Timing Below 15° Latitude – 27
   Field Harvest Timing Below 15° Latitude – 28

2. **Plant Propagation** – 33

   Choosing a Propagation Method – 33
   Growing Media – 38
   Starting Stevia from Seed – 39
   Propagating Stevia from Stem Cuttings – 44
   Propagating Stevia with Crown Divisions – 53
   Breeding through Selection – 54

3. **Field Preparation and Plant Care** – 57

   Field Location – 57
   Soils and Fertilization – 58
   Field Tillage – 65
   Irrigation – 68
   Mulching – 70
   Weed Control – 77
   Row Covers – 78
   Plant Pruning – 82
   Nutrient Deficiencies and Toxicities – 85
   Pests and Diseases – 86

4. **Field Planting** – 93

   Planting Density – 93
   Transplanting to the Field – 100

5. **Harvesting and Postharvest** – 103

   Cutting and Gathering – 104
   Drying Stevia Leaves – 110
   Separating Leaves from Stems – 116
   Leaf Storage and Shipping – 121

6. **Marketing and Economics** – 123

   Enterprise Budgeting – 124
   Selling Dried Leaves Wholesale – 125
   Dry Leaf Yields from Small-Scale Trials – 130
   Dry Leaf Yields from Large-Scale Trials – 131
   Selling Dried Leaves Retail – 132
   Selling Stevia Plants – 133
   Fresh Stevia Leaves – 136
   On-Farm Processing – 138

Appendix 1: Field Trial Summaries – 141

Appendix 2: Stevia Leaf Buyers – 167

Appendix 3: Selected Resources – 169

Glossary – 179

Bibliography – 187

Index – 193

About the Author – 205

Figures

1. Magnified stevia leaves and seeds – 4
2. Stevia blossoms – 5
3. Plant sprouting back from crown in spring – 15
4. Blossoming stevia plants – 18
5. Day length at various latitudes – 20
6. Last spring freeze dates in the US – 30
7. First fall freeze dates in the US – 31
8. Dry leaf yield by propagation method – 38
9. Stevia seeds – 39
10. Nursery flat with cell-pack inserts – 40
11. Newly sprouted stevia seedlings – 41
12. Young plants from seed in cell packs – 43
13. Growing stevia plants from stem cuttings – 44
14. Plants from stem cuttings – 46
15. Potted plants under fluorescent light in winter – 50
16. Stevia plant crowns being put into cold storage – 51
17. Multi-stem stevia plant that could be divided – 52
18. Dry leaf yield by fertilization treatment – 60
19. Dry leaf yield by nitrogen fertilization level – 62
20. Dry leaf yield by fertilization level in India – 63
21. Small raised growing beds – 65
22. Stevia in raised beds with overhead irrigation – 67
23. Stevia plant with rubber drip hose – 70
24. Dry leaf yield with black plastic mulch versus no mulch – 73
25. Dry leaf yield & income difference using black plastic mulch – 74
26. Dry leaf yield under plastic high tunnels versus open field – 81
27. Yield and gross income differences using plastic high tunnels – 82
28. Plants branching after pruning – 84

29. Dry leaf yield per plant by planting density – 94
30. Dry leaf yield & income difference using high planting density – 96
31. Plant spacing options, unit conversions, and yields – 98
32. Dry leaf yield at various planting densities in a tropical climate – 99
33. Young stevia plants grown on raised beds – 100
34. Stevia blossoms and blossom buds – 104
35. HT-Cala Harvester from Jenquip – 107
36. Jenquip herb harvester with infeed reel – 108
37. Dried stevia leaves on and off stems – 111
38. Dried stevia leaves in a food dehydrator – 113
39. Hang drying stevia –114
40. Advertised dried stevia leaf prices – 129
41. Making green stevia powder in a food processor – 138
42. Green stevia powder, whole leaf, and white extract – 140

Acknowledgments

I am especially grateful to my friend and mentor, the late Dr. Alejandro Ching. As a professor of plant science at Northwest Missouri State University, he was growing, researching, and promoting stevia before I ever heard about it. In 1998, Dr. Ching gave me the chance to conduct a research project dealing with seed germination in stevia.[1] Dr. Ching was energetic, positive, and full of enthusiasm, especially about his faith and about plants that could help farmers and consumers.

My thanks to Steve Marsden of Herbal Advantage Inc. for sharing wisdom gleaned from years of growing, buying, and selling stevia. I would also like to thank Dr. Clinton Shock for reviewing the manuscript. Dr. Shock is a pioneer in stevia cultivation research and continues working with stevia.

Many people have helped me become a better writer and better person over the years. I am grateful to all of them.

---

[1] Jeffrey Goettemoeller and Alejandro Ching, "Seed Germination in Stevia rebaudiana," in J. Janick, ed., *Perspectives on new crops and new uses* (Alexandria, VA: ASHS Press, 1999) 510–511.
http://www.hort.purdue.edu/newcrop/proceedings1999/v4-510.html.

Preface

Governments around the world are approving stevia for wider use in food and beverage products. In the United States, sales of stevia leaves, extracts, and powdered leaf have long been allowed under the 1994 Dietary Supplement Health and Education Act (DSHEA).[2] More recently, the US Food and Drug Administration (FDA) has approved certain stevia extracts for use as food additives. Elsewhere, the Joint FAO/WHO Expert Committee on Food Additives (JECFA) and the European Food Safety Authority (EFSA) have issued positive opinions on the safety of glycosides from stevia for use as food additives.[3] This could lead to widespread approval in the European Union. Clearly, the time for expanded stevia production has arrived.

Stevia rebaudiana thrives in a wide variety of climates and soils. It can be a perennial crop in some climates or an annual crop where winters are cold. However, the cultivation of stevia is fairly new.[4] We've only begun to optimize procedures for commercial production. There is great potential for improvement in stevia yield, quality, and profits. This book provides a head start for academic and on-farm experimentation. Best practices for stevia cultivation are suggested based

---

[2] See Rob McCaleb, "Controversial Products in the Natural Foods Market," The Herb Research Foundation: Herb Information Greenpaper, 1997. http://www.herbs.org/greenpapers/controv.html (accessed 7-29-2010).

[3] See Elaine Watson, "EFSA opinion paves way for EU approval of stevia-based sweeteners," Foodnavigator.com, April 14, 2010.

[4] For a succinct history of stevia use and cultivation, see W.H. Lewis, "Early uses of Stevia rebaudiana (Asteraceae) leaves as a sweetener in Paraguay," *Economic Botany* 46 (1992): 336–337.

on research studies from around the world as well as the author's own experience of growing and using stevia for over a decade. *Growing Stevia for Market* will help farmers, researchers, market gardeners, nurseries, and greenhouse operators succeed with stevia.

For your convenience, web site addresses are given in the appendix and in many of the footnotes throughout this book. Some of these web sites may be moved or discontinued over time. For updated links and other updated information, visit the author's stevia web site at:

www.growingstevia.com

Good Growing!

Introduction

Stevia as an Alternative Crop

Stevia rebaudiana is probably the sweetest plant on earth. Whole dried leaves taste about 12–15 times sweeter than cane sugar. Extracts of stevia's sweet glycosides can taste up to 300 times sweeter than sugar. Yet stevia leaves are low-glycemic (slow to cause blood sugar swings), very low in calories,[5] and do not promote dental cavities.[6] One of the best research-based sources for information on the safety and efficacy of stevia is the European Stevia Center at:

> http://bio.kuleuven.be/biofys/ESC/ESC.htm

Stevia's glycosides are well suited for use in food and beverage products. An author writing for Foodnavigator.com indicates some of the advantages of Rebaudioside A (one of stevia's glycosides) as a food additive: "Unlike some other high-intensity sweeteners, Reb-A is light, heat and acid stable,

---

[5] A 2004 study confirmed stevia leaf is lower in calories than aspartame, much sweeter than sucrose, and has a lower glycemic index as compared to sucrose. See S.M. Savita and others, "Stevia rebaudiana—A Functional Component for Food Industry," *Journal of Human Ecology* 15, no. 4 (2004): 261–264.

[6] A University Of Illinois College Of Dentistry study found that neither Stevioside nor Rebaudioside A (the main sweet glycosides in stevia) was cariogenic (promoting of dental cavities) under the conditions of the study. See S. A. Das and others, "Evaluation of the Cariogenic Potential of the Intense Natural Sweeteners Stevioside and Rebaudioside A," *Caries Research* 26, no. 5 (1992): 363.

which makes it ideal for acidic juice drinks and pasteurised dairy products."[7]

With our craving for sweet treats, it is easy to see the potential of stevia as a commercial crop. Benefits of expanded stevia production could extend to the environment, economy, and farm income. Currently, sugar cane and corn syrup dominate the world sweetener market. Sugar cane and field corn occupy some of our best farmland. By shifting partially to stevia, we could free up these fields for production of other food products, biofuels, or other bioproducts.

Large-scale trials conducted by Kansas State University (US) resulted in a stevia dry leaf yield of 3285 lb/acre under irrigation.[8] Assuming dried stevia leaves have 12 times the sweetening power of sugar, that acre of stevia would produce the sweetening equivalent of about 39,420 lb. sugar. This is about seven times the average per-acre yield of Louisiana sugar cane in 2004.[9] In other words, an acre of Kansas stevia could replace the sweetening power of seven acres of Louisiana sugar cane. Those seven acres of sugar cane could then be turned into about 2669 gal. of high octane ethanol fuel.[10] This is a conservative estimate of stevia's potential as a crop. Large-scale stevia cultivation is still in its infancy. New stevia varie-

---

[7] Elaine Watson, "EFSA opinion paves way for EU approval of stevia-based sweeteners," Foodnavigator.com, April 14, 2010.

[8] Rhonda Janke, *Farming a Few Acres of Herbs: Stevia* (Kansas State University, 2004). http://www.ksre.ksu.edu/ksherbs/stevia.htm.

[9] Based on a sugar yield of 5527 pounds per harvested acre of sugar cane as reported by the Louisiana State University AgCenter web site in 2010. http://www.lsuagcenter.com.

[10] Based on deriving 135.4 gallons of ethanol per short ton of raw sugar as reported in Hosein Shapouri and Michael Salassi, "The Economic Feasibility of Ethanol Production from Sugar in the United States," USDA (July 2006). http://www.usda.gov/oce/reports/energy/EthanolSugarFeasibilityReport3.pdf.

ties and improvements in agronomic practices will lift yields much higher. Based on small-scale trials at Davis, California, researcher Clinton Shock estimated an acre of stevia could yield the sweetening power equivalent of 56,000 lb. sucrose sugar.[11] This would represent 10 acres of Louisiana sugar cane.

Sugar cane and field corn require fertile soils and long, warm growing seasons. Stevia can produce good yields on soils and in climates not suited for standard row crops, and with far fewer pesticides and less fertilization per unit of sweetening power.

In some cases, stevia could replace crops such as tobacco and opium poppy. The soils, climate, equipment, and production skills needed for these crops could be applied to stevia. A study in Greece found stevia has low fertilization and pesticide requirements, and shows good potential for replacing tobacco as a farm crop. The study also found the irrigation requirements for stevia are 30%–40% of those for tobacco.[12] Conducted by the University of Thessaly, this study involved large-scale trials in multiple regions of Greece.

About the Stevia Plant

Stevia rebaudiana Bertoni is in the Asteraceae/Compositae family,[13] same as sunflowers, marigolds, lettuce, zinnia, daisies, and asters. The most notable feature of stevia is the

---

[11] Clinton C. Shock, "Rebaudi's Stevia: natural noncaloric sweeteners," *California Agriculture*, September–October 1982.

[12] Επιμέλεια: Αλίκη Φωτιάδου. "Κερδίζει έδαφος στη Θεσσαλία η καλλιέργεια της στέβιας." TAHYDROMOS, 2009. [Alice Fotiadou, ed., "Gaining ground in Thessaly growing Stevia"]

[13] For more information on the taxonomy of stevia, see the USDA ARS Germplasm Resources Information Network at http://www.ars-grin.gov/cgi-bin/npgs/html/taxon.pl?35581#syn.

surprising sweetness of the leaves. These leaves are usually 1–3 in. (25–76 mm) in length. Stems are stiff, brittle, and non-woody. With older plants, several stems sprout from a central crown. Plants often reach 24–30 in. (61–76 cm) in height under cultivation. Different genotypes (distinct genetic lines) exhibit varied leaf shapes, leaf size, plant size, and growth habits. The two leaves shown in figure 1, for instance, are from two different genotypes.

Plants grown from seed will have some genetic variation from plant to plant. Asexual propagation (such as stem cuttings) will better preserve the genetic composition of the plant from one generation to the next.

Figure 1: Magnified stevia leaves and seeds.

Stevia rebaudiana is native to Paraguay in subtropical South America. Stevia is a tender perennial, surviving year-round outdoors only where winters are mild. Unprotected plants do not usually survive prolonged temperatures below 25°F (–4° Celsius). Fortunately, stevia thrives as an annual, replanted every year. This usually means only one harvest is taken per year. But in high latitudes, the yield from that one harvest is likely to be good. Long summer days encourage greater leaf growth and a higher concentration of sweet glycoside molecules.

In the wild, stevia tends to grow where the soil is usually moist, but not waterlogged, and high in organic matter. It reproduces through reseeding, natural layering (stems fall to the ground and strike root) or by crown division (multiple stems sprouting from plant crown). Shoots usually die after maturing or from frost. New shoots arise by tillering from the plant base. Tiny white blossoms are produced in profusion and pollinated by wind or insects. Often, stevia seeds produced by wild plants are not viable.[14] However, good stevia seeds with a high germination rate are now available commercially. Stevia seeds are tiny and slender, similar to lettuce seeds.

Figure 2: Stevia blossoms.

---

[14] For a description of stevia growing wild, see Shock, "Rebaudi's Stevia"

Chapter 1

Climate and Day Length

Patterns of temperature, rainfall, and sunlight influence most aspects of stevia cultivation. In this chapter, we consider how climate and day length affect stevia yield as well as the timing and frequency of planting and harvesting. Field production cycles can range from a single growing season for annual production to several years for perennial production.

Plant Hardiness Zones

This book makes reference to "USDA Plant Hardiness Zones." More specifically, I am relying on the 1990 version of the USDA Plant Hardiness Zone map. The USDA web site explains how these zones are determined:

> This 1990 version shows in detail the lowest temperatures that can be expected each year in the United States, Canada, and Mexico. These temperatures are referred to as "average annual minimum temperatures" and are based on the lowest temperatures recorded for each of the years

1974 to 1986 in the United States and Canada and 1971 to 1984 in Mexico.[15]

In North America, find your USDA Plant Hardiness Zone by using the map on this web site:

www.usna.usda.gov/Hardzone/ushzmap.html

Plant hardiness maps have been produced for many regions of the world, often based on the USDA Plant Hardiness Zones. Many of these maps can be found on the internet with a search for "plant hardiness zone" followed by the nation or region in which you are interested. Also find links to some of these maps at my stevia web site:

www.growingstevia.com

Perennial or Annual Production

Stevia rebaudiana is classified as a tender perennial. This means it will survive through the winter without protection only where temperatures remain sufficiently warm. Perennial production is usually preferred because it avoids the cost of yearly planting. Annual production (replanting every year) is a viable option where perennial production is not possible.

If your average annual minimum winter temperature is above 30°F (1.2°C), perennial production with year-round growth is likely feasible, even if you experience occasional frosts or freezes. This corresponds to USDA Plant Hardiness Zone 10 or above. Based on my observations, mature plants

---

[15] United States National Arboretum, "Introduction to the USDA Plant Hardiness Zone Map." http://www.usna.usda.gov/Hardzone/index.html (accessed July 2, 2010).

can withstand temperatures down to at least 28°F (−2.2°C) without significant leaf damage. Even if plant tops are damaged from unusually cold temperatures, the roots will often survive and sprout back. Mulch aides root survival at colder temperatures. Even where temperatures never drop below freezing, winter plant growth may cease or slow because of shorter day lengths and cooler temperatures. Typically, stevia plants under perennial production are allowed to grow 3–5 years. Yields tend to diminish after a few years. In the state of Orissa, India (about lat 20°N), farmers reported acceptable yields for three years.[16]

Mulching can facilitate perennial production (with winter dormancy) in somewhat colder climates than would otherwise be possible. Under an eight-inch deep straw and leaf mulch topped with black plastic, I have had a few plants survive Missouri winter temperatures as low as 10°F (−12°C). Tops had been harvested and plants went into a dormant state, then sprouted back in the spring after mulch was removed. However, winter survival is not sufficiently consistent for commercial production here in USDA Plant Hardiness Zone 5.

I have found that stevia plant roots may be dug after harvest and kept in cold storage at 33°F–55°F over the winter, buried in moist dirt or sand (much like storing root crops). If all goes well, plants sprout back when replanted in the spring. But this is a very labor intensive method of maintaining plants on a perennial basis.

In trials near Bonn, Germany, researchers tried unheated high tunnels (plastic-covered hoops over multiple beds) for

---

[16] Kalpana Rayaguru and K Khan Md., "Post-harvest management of stevia leaves: A review," *Journal of Food Science and Technology* 45, no. 5 (2008): 395.

winter protection.¹⁷ Plants did not survive, even though winters in the region tend to be somewhat warmer than in northern Missouri. This failure of perennial production might have been due to added warmth in tunnels during the day, spurring faster plant growth. Active growth might make plants more susceptible to cold winter nights.

In cold-winter climates, clear row covers (low tunnels) or high tunnels could be used to get a faster start in the spring, but probably will not aide winter survival. Rather, plants need to be allowed to enter a dormant state (with little or no top growth) for a better chance at survival.

---

[17] R. Pude, M. Schmitz-Eiberger, and G. Noga, "Development, Yield and Selected Contents of Stevia rebaudiana," *Zeitschrift F☐uur Arznei- & Gewuurzpflanzen* 10 (2005): 37–43.

Choosing a Stevia Field Production Cycle

- **Perennial field production with year-round top growth:**
Locations with an average annual minimum temperature of 30°F (−1.2°C) or warmer. This corresponds to USDA Plant Hardiness Zone 10 or above. US cities in this category include Naples, Florida; Victorville, California; Miami, Florida; Coral Gables, Florida; and Honolulu, Hawaii. Tropical and some sub-tropical regions around the world can support this type of production.

- **Perennial production with winter dormancy:**
Marginal locations with an average annual minimum temperature between 10°F (−12.2°C) and 30°F (−1.2°C). This corresponds to USDA Plant Hardiness Zones 8 and 9. US cities in this category include Tifton, Georgia; Dallas, Texas; Austin, Texas; Gainesville, Florida; Houston, Texas; St. Augustine, Florida; Brownsville, Texas; and Fort Pierce, Florida.

- **Annual field production** (replanting every year):
For locations with an average minimum temperature of 10°F (−12.2°C) or colder. This corresponds to USDA Plant Hardiness Zone 7 or colder, which includes continental climates in much of the US, Canada, Northern Europe, Asia, and elsewhere.

Perennial Production with Winter Dormancy

In marginal climates (with somewhat cold winters), perennial production with winter dormancy may be possible. Cessation of top growth after shoot maturation is normal in stevia's native range.[18] Where the average minimum tempera-

---

[18] See Shock, "Rebaudi's Stevia"

ture is between 10°F (−4°C) and 30°F (−1.2°C), I suggest trying perennial production with winter dormancy. These temperatures correspond to USDA Plant Hardiness Zones 8 and 9. If this method of overwintering proves reliable, you could increase the perennial portion of your crop. This would save the cost of yearly replanting. It would also give plants a head-start on spring growth.

Reports have been made of stevia plants routinely surviving above-ground winter die-back under field conditions. During the winters of 1979–1980 and 1980–1981, stevia plants in Davis, California (lat 38.5°N) survived despite die-back of tops from frost.[19] After overwintering, tops grew back beginning in March, though survival was threatened by slug damage. Davis is located near Sacramento, in USDA Plant Hardiness Zone 9b.

In 2002, stevia was planted in North-West Tasmania.[20] Tops died back completely in the winter. The presence of sclerotinia and other diseases led to the death of many plants, but some survived through the winter and sprouted back in the spring. The climate in this region is probably equivalent to USDA Plant Hardiness Zone 9.

Near Pisa, Italy (lat 43.7°N), trials conducted from 1992 through 2000 showed the reliability of perennial production

---

[19] Clinton C. Shock, "Experimental Cultivation of Rebaudi's Stevia in California," *Agronomy Progress Report #122*, University of California, Davis Agricultural Experiment Station, April 1982.

[20] Phillip Wilk and Wendy Dingle, ed., *Proceedings of the 3rd National Herb, Native Foods and Essential Oils convention, workshops and farm visits 14th–16th August, 2003, Lismore, NSW.* RIRDC Publication No 04/059 Project No TA 023-36. (Rural Industries Research and Development Corporation, 2004), 58.

with winter dormancy.[21] This region is in the equivalent of USDA Plant Hardiness Zone 9, with a Mediterranean climate.[22]

In India, researchers at the AKS Herbal Research and Land Development Centre (Uttar Pradesh), found their winters to be a little too cold for reliable winter stevia survival. But stevia plants survived better through the winter by temporarily covering crowns of plants during those nights when temperatures dropped below 5°C (41°F).[23]

At Palampur, Himachal Pradesh, India (lat 32°N), stevia plants survived winter die-back of tops and grew back in the spring without the need for covering.

> With the onset of winter in November, growth of the plants ceased. The crop was frost-susceptible and withered due to frost injury in January. Dead biomass was removed from all the plots during the end of February 2002. Vigorous crop regeneration was observed during onset of spring (first week of March) from the underground root crowns.[24]

In many places, stevia survives winter in a dormant state without the need for mulch. But mulch can help expand the range where perennial production is possible. A plastic film covering may be used if it is just temporary and only during the night. During the day, a plastic covering might cause

---

[21] Laura Andolfi, Mario Macchia and Lucia Ceccarini, "Agronomic-productive Characteristics of Two Genotype of Stevia Rebaudiana in Central Italy," *Ital. J. Agron. / Riv. Agron.* 1, no. 2 (2006): 257–263.

[22] See map at http://www.uk.gardenweb.com/forums/zones/hze6.html (accessed July 2, 2010).

[23] S.D. Singh and G.P. Rao, "Stevia: The Herbal Sugar of 21st Century," *Sugar Tech* 7, no. 1 (2005): 17–24.

[24] N. W. Megeji, J. K. Kumar, V. Singh, V. K. Kaul, and P. S. Ahuja, "Introducing Stevia rebaudiana, a natural zero-calorie sweetener," *Current Science* 88, no. 5 (2005): 802.

warming and premature top growth. In colder climates, mulch will need to remain in place through much of the winter. In this case, it should be an organic mulch (such as straw) rather than plastic. The goal is to keep roots cold, but not frozen. A thick layer of organic mulch (4–6 in. or 10–15 cm) will protect plant roots from freezing during the winter. Plastic sheets could go on top of the organic mulch, but this will probably not be necessary in most cases.

For mulched perennial production in marginal climates, transplant plugs (young plants) to the field after all danger of frost in the spring, preferably after day lengths begin to exceed 13 hours (see section on day length below). In hot climates, apply four inches (10 cm) of straw mulch (or other organic mulch) around the plants when the weather begins to heat up.

At harvest time, cut whole stems at 4–6 in. (10–15 cm) above ground level. Due to short winter day lengths and colder temperatures, plants will likely grow slowly, if at all, during the fall and winter. Plants will be in a semi-dormant state, more resistant to frosts and freezes. If growth occurs and foliage is damaged by a freeze, prune away damaged stems. Plant crowns may still be alive and capable of sending up new shoots. Before freezing temperatures arrive, add more mulch over plants to 4–6 in. (10–15 cm) deep.

Organic mulch might encourage slug damage on young spring shoots. Plants should be watched closely. Mulch could be removed in the spring to reduce slug damage and allow for warming of the soil.

Figure 3: Plant sprouting back from crown in spring.

Photoperiod and Leaf Yield

Photoperiod is the duration of a plant's exposure to light in every 24-hour period. A more common term for photoperiod is "day length." But the light need not come from the sun. Artificial lighting can be used to provide a particular photoperiod.

Most *Stevia rebaudiana* genotypes are "short-day." This means blossoming is triggered when plants are exposed to sufficiently short days (or you could say "long enough nights") over a sufficiently long number of days. I have seen only one strain that appeared to be "long-day" (blossoming triggered under long-day conditions).

For maximum leaf production, blossoming should be discouraged. A longer period of leaf growth uninterrupted by blossoming will result in larger leaf and glycoside yields. As with most plants, resources are re-directed toward seed production and away from leaf production as blossoming proceeds. Therefore, it is generally best to harvest a stevia crop when the first blossom buds form.

Sunshine and Glycoside Content

The effect of day length and exposure to sunlight goes beyond blossom timing. Studies show longer days promote not only greater leaf yield, but also higher glycoside concentrations in stevia leaves.[25] Glycosides are the sweet molecules in stevia leaves. Stevioside is one of the main glycosides in stevia plants. A Brazilian study showed that quality and intensity of light (not just photoperiod) is important for stevioside content. Researchers exposed one group of stevia plants to eight hours of artificial lighting per day and another group to eight hours of natural sunlight. Plants exposed to natural sunlight produced leaves with a higher stevioside content.[26] "Thus, it seems that the content of stevioside is related to the total irradiance received by the plant rather than the photoperiod itself."[27]

Simply put, longer days and shorter nights are better for stevia leaf production. This is why annual production at mid and high latitude locations can be profitable despite the cost of

---

[25] See Jacques Metivier and Ana Maria Viana, "The Effect of Long and Short day Length upon the Growth of Whole Plants and the Level of Soluble Proteins, Sugars, and Stevioside in Leaves of Stevia rebaudiana Bert.," *Journal of Experimental Botany* 30, no. 119 (1979) 1211–1222.

[26] Zaidan, Dietrich, and Felippe, "Effect of photoperiod on flowering and stevioside content in plants of Stevia rebaudiana Bertoni," *Jap. J. Crop Sci.* 49 (1980): 569–574.

[27] Ibid.

yearly planting and the limitation of only one or two harvests per year. The longer summer days at higher latitudes induce faster leaf growth and greater glycoside concentration as compared to lower latitudes (closer to the equator) where summer days are shorter. On the other hand, perennial production and year-round growth are often possible in lower-latitude locations.

The highest-latitude regions with warm enough winters for perennial production might be expected to provide the optimum conditions for profitable stevia production. Typically, these are coastal areas where temperatures are moderated by large bodies of water. In one way or another, though, it seems stevia can be a profitable crop in a wide range of locations around the world.

Stevia's Critical Day Length for Blossoming

For a plant like stevia, the "critical day length" is the photoperiod that triggers blossoming. While the exact number varies depending on factors such as genotype, the critical day length for *Stevia rebaudiana* is usually about 13 hours. This means blossoming will be triggered when a plant is exposed to less than 13 hours of light per 24-hour period over several days. More accurately speaking, blossoming is triggered when the plants are exposed to 11 or more hours of continuous darkness per 24-hour period (a critical dark period of 11 hours).

For the purposes of optimum stevia leaf growth and glycoside content, we want to avoid blossoming. For most genotypes, this means exposing plants to 13 or more hours of daylight throughout the growing season. This is especially important for the timing of transplanting to the field. If possible, transplanting should occur as days are growing longer in the spring.

Figure 4: Blossoming stevia plants.

There appears to be potential for selecting stevia genotypes with delayed blossoming at various day lengths. In one study, researchers were able to identify a few genotypes that exhibited minimal blossoming for a longer period of time as compared to other genotypes.[28]

---

[28] Ibid.

Determining Day Length

Day length is mostly determined by latitude. Based on your latitude, you can determine day length for any time of the year. Here's how:

1. Find your latitude using a globe or one of the map tools at these web sites:

   www.earthtools.org
   www.esrl.noaa.gov/gmd/grad/solcalc/

2. Use the graph in figure 5 to determine your approximate day length throughout the year. Use the latitude line closest to your own latitude. You could also visit this web site with day length tables for various latitudes:

   www.orchidculture.com/COD/daylength.html

At the equator, day length is 12 hours throughout the year. As you move away from the equator, summer day lengths are longer and winter day lengths are shorter.

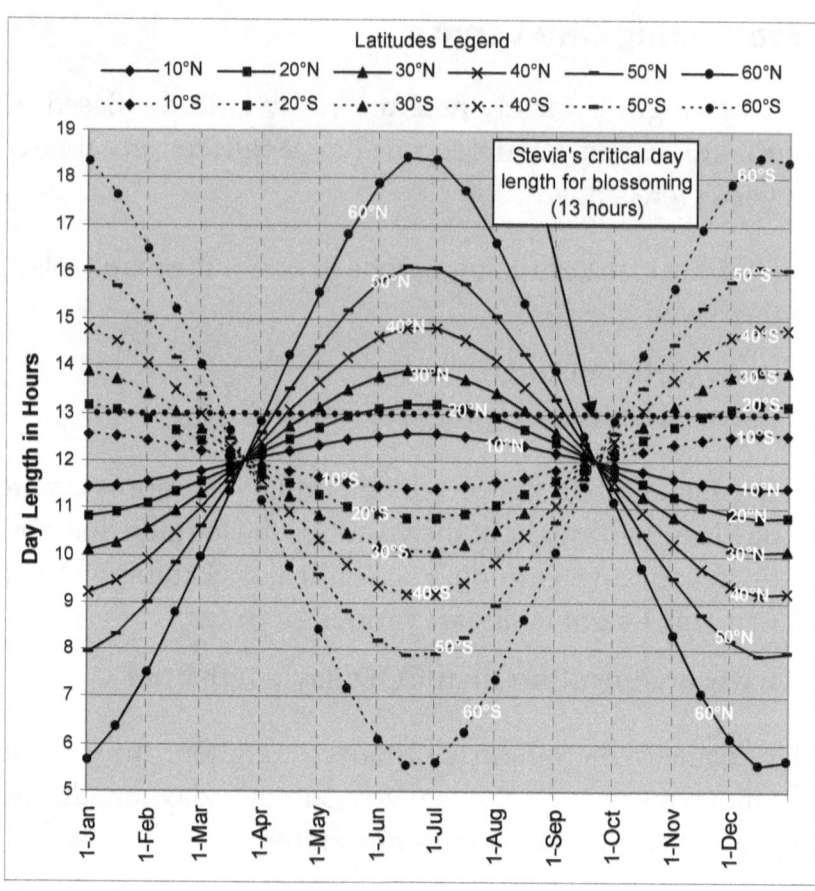

Figure 5: Day length at various latitudes.[29]
Day lengths less than about 13 hours trigger blossoming in most stevia strains. Transplanting to the field in the spring (when day lengths are increasing) encourages leaf growth. Blossom buds usually appear 2–3 weeks after day lengths drop below 13 hours in the fall.

---

[29]Day length data from "Day Lengths for Various Latitudes," http://www.orchidculture.com/COD/daylength.html#40N.

Field Transplant Timing Above 15° Latitude

Above 15° latitude in either hemisphere, transplanting to the field should generally be done as early in the spring as temperatures allow, but not before April 15 in the northern hemisphere or October 15 in the southern hemisphere. This will ensure long and lengthening days, best for leaf growth.

At High Latitudes with Mild Winters

Areas of northern California in USDA Hardiness Zones 8 or above would be examples of locations where day length (rather than temperature) would dictate how early you would transplant to the field. In this area, relatively high latitudes are combined with relatively warm winter temperatures because of the moderating effect of the Pacific ocean. At latitudes around 40°N and above, day lengths vary widely from winter to summer. Therefore it might be a good idea to wait until April 15 for field transplanting so that young plants get the best possible start, taking advantage of the long and lengthening days on that date.

Field transplanting dates would be dictated by day length in many areas of Europe as well, or any high-latitude region with moderate temperatures. In these regions, stevia benefits from long summer days combined with mild winter temperatures. An early spring transplanting date takes best advantage of the long day lengths.

In some mild-winter locations, factors such as high air temperature may make an even earlier transplanting date advisable despite shorter day lengths. Extremely hot temperatures in desert and Mediterranean climates can impede establishment of newly transplanted plants. In Giza, Egypt (about lat 30°N), researchers transplanted stevia to the field at the beginning of April. The first cutting was taken 90 days later. About 40%–56% of the plants were blossoming at the time of harvest.[30] But mild winters at Giza allow for year-round growth. The cumulative yield (from five harvests per year) was quite good despite the blossoming at harvest time.

At High Latitudes with Cold Winters

Where winters are cold, transplanting to the field will need to wait until at least after all danger of frost. Ideally, average daily low temperatures should be above 55°F (12.8°C) and average soil temperature at the 2–4 in. depth should be above 65°F (18.3°C). Cool soil and air temperatures, even if above freezing, will slow growth of young stevia plants. Mature, overwintered plants may be transplanted to the field somewhat earlier because they tolerate colder temperatures.

By modifying soil and air temperatures, the temperature-determined growing season may be lengthened somewhat. Black plastic mulch may be used to boost soil temperatures, while row covers can boost air and soil temperatures early in the season. But day length must also be considered. It will not pay to push planting dates very early if day lengths are too short.

As a general rule, transplant stevia to the field 1–3 weeks after the "10% probability" freeze-free date at your location, as long as this is not before April 15 (Northern hemisphere) or October 15 (Southern hemisphere). The "10% probability" freeze-free date is the date after which there is only a 10% chance of dropping to 32°F (0°C) or below. The National

---

[30] A. E. Attia, O. H. El-Bagoury, A. I. Allam, and A. M. A. Elghany, "Effect of Propagation Method and Nitrogen Fertilization on Stevia (Stevia Rebaudiana Bertoni) Yield and Quality in Egypt," *Egyptian Journal of Agricultural Research* 83, no. 3 (2005): 1269–1292.

Climatic Data Center (NCDC) publishes these dates for hundreds of locations across the United States, based on historical observations. Click on "Frost/Freeze Data 1971–2000" at this web site:

http://cdo.ncdc.noaa.gov/cgi-bin/climatenormals/climatenormals.pl

First-freeze dates for the fall are included in the database as well. Mature stevia foliage will generally withstand temperatures a few degrees below freezing. Figures 6 and 7 are freeze occurrence maps for the United States. Data for these maps are older—collected from 1951 through 1980. Nonetheless, they give some guidance about earliest possible transplanting dates and latest possible harvest dates based on temperature.

Temperatures will vary from one field to the next and from one season to the next. Also use your local forecast and temperature readings from your field to determine the best field transplanting date—that date when nighttime temperatures will remain mostly above 45°F (7.2°C).

My hometown of Maryville, Missouri (lat 40°N and USDA Plant Hardiness Zone 5a) is an example of a location where cold spring temperatures are the limiting factor in how early stevia can be transplanted to the field unprotected. At 40°N latitude, day lengths rise above 13 hours around mid April (see fig. 5). But the NCDC web site shows the 10% probability date for an occurrence of 32°F (0°C) is May 5. Therefore I should generally wait until at least May 12 (a week after May 5) to put plants in the field unprotected.

Row covers (plastic low tunnels or high tunnels) may extend the season up to about two weeks earlier, taking advantage of long spring days at higher latitudes. In Maryville, then, row covers may allow transplanting to the field as early as April 28 (about a week before May 5). Row covers or individual "hot caps" can protect against unexpected late frosts. But beware of overheating. Vent or remove covers as needed.

Warmer temperatures under row covers would tend to speed early growth in cool climates, even when they are not needed for frost protection. In a trial near Bonn, Germany (lat 50.6°N) leaf yields were higher with high tunnels (plastic-covered hoops over multiple beds) compared to no covers in annual production.[31] The yield increase was 25%–43%. On-farm trials can determine whether row covers give a good return on investment at your location. For a valid comparison, make sure other variables are the same. Results will vary from season to season because of changing variables such as weather. During very hot growing seasons, plastic covers will probably not provide as much advantage. Covers should be vented or removed when hot temperatures arrive.

Field Harvest Timing Above 15° Latitude

Trials in the Czech Republic (lat about 50°N) resulted in the highest yield of stevioside per plant (131 mg) by harvesting in early September, a few weeks before blossoming.[32] At higher latitudes, blossoming is likely to begin 2–3 weeks after day lengths drop below 13 hours. As a general rule, the crop should be harvested as the first blossom buds appear. Weather conditions might dictate the precise harvest date. Where

---

[31] Pude, Schmitz-Eiberger, and Noga, "Development, Yield"

[32] A. Nepovim, H. Drahosova, P. Valicek, and T. Vanek, "The effect of cultivation conditions on the content of stevioside in Stevia rebaudiana Bertoni plants cultivated in the Czech Republic," *Pharmaceutical and Pharmacological Letters* 8, no. 1 (1998): 19–21.

climate allows, plants might then re-grow until the next blossoming. Otherwise, plants will go dormant or die from cold winter temperatures. In Maryville, Missouri, US (lat 40°N), day lengths drop to 13 hours around the beginning of September. Harvest time arrives in late September when blossom buds begin to form. Because of cold winters, the September harvest generally marks the end for my plants unless I dig some to overwinter indoors.

In cases where the long-day, frost-free growing season is over five months, a mid-summer harvest might be advisable even when blossoming has not yet occurred. Then a second harvest can be taken when blossom buds first appear in the fall. For instance, total annual dry leaf yield near Pisa, Italy (lat 43.7°N) was greater with two harvests per year as compared to one.[33] This is a Mediterranean climate with a very long growing season, long summer days, and cool winters. The production cycle is perennial with winter dormancy.

The normal planting date in warmer regions of Northern California (about lat 40°N or above) would be about April 15. If blossoms do not appear until fall, there would normally be just one fall harvest. But with this 5+ month growing season under long-day conditions, you might get a larger overall yield by harvesting in mid-summer and again in late September. It might also result in higher quality leaves. Disease and dirt may eventually damage older leaves the longer plants are allowed to grow before harvest. Plants should be monitored to judge whether they are growing fast enough for a mid-summer harvest.

---

[33] Andolfi, Macchia, and Ceccarini, "Agronomic-productive"

Where Winters are Mild

In regions allowing winter top growth, winter harvests may be possible. This is more likely feasible the closer you get to the equator, because winter day lengths will be longer. Winter blossoming might be continuous, so harvests must be done during the early stage of blossoming. In Giza, Egypt (lat about 30°N), researchers harvested stevia five times per year, spread throughout the entire year (including winter).[34] Blossoming was well under way at the time of each cutting. This tends to reduce leaf growth. Because of year-round growth, however, total dry leaf yield for the year was good.

In a location above about 40° latitude (north or south), winter growth may be poor despite mild winters. This is because of short winter day lengths at those latitudes. But plant roots will likely survive the winter and grow back stronger in the spring. Side-by-side trials can be used to determine which harvest schedule will produce the highest profit on your farm.

Where Cold Temperatures Determine Harvest Timing

Even where growing seasons are short, stevia might be profitable because of rapid growth and high yields spurred by long summer days at high latitudes. Mature stevia tops will survive temperatures a few degrees below freezing. In fact, Canadian researcher Mike Columbus found that mature plants will survive temperatures as low as 21.2°F (−6°C) in the fall.[35] At very high latitudes or high altitudes, however, cold temperature might force a harvest before blossoming does so.

---

[34] Attia et al., "Effect of Propagation Method and Nitrogen"
[35] Mike Columbus (Ontario Ministry of Agriculture), "Stevia," in Rita Berzins, Helen Snell, and Conrad Richter, eds., *Richters Second Commercial Herb Growing Conference* (Goodwood, Ontario: Richters, 1998) 5.

Freezing temperatures might arrive before days grow short enough to trigger formation of blossom buds. In this case, harvest the crop before your first hard freeze. See figure 7 to get an idea of first fall freeze dates in the United States, or visit the National Climatic Data Center at the link listed earlier.

In North America, consider northern Minnesota, North Dakota, Montana, and nearby areas of Canada. In this cold continental climate, freezing temperatures would usually force harvesting by early September. This is prior to the usual appearance of blossom buds at that latitude (near 50°N). At 50°N latitude, day lengths drop below 13 hours in early September (see fig. 5). The first blossom buds could be expected 2–3 weeks later, around the end of September.

Field Transplant Timing Below 15° Latitude

Close to the equator (between lat 15°N and 15°S), day length never exceeds 13 hours. Under these year-round short-day conditions, stevia will blossom at about 54–104 days after transplanting (depending on factors such as the photoperiod sensitivity of the genotype), no matter the time of year.[36] Therefore, day length will not be a big a factor in field transplant timing. Temperature and rainfall patterns may be more important. Flooding rains, temperatures over 90°F (32.2°C), or drought can inhibit establishment of young plants. Raised growing beds, shading, or irrigation can mitigate those factors, but it is better if nature cooperates.

---

[36] See K. Ramesh, V. Singh, and N. W. Megeji, "Cultivation of Stevia [Stevia rebaudiana (Bert.) Bertoni]: A Comprehensive Review," *Advances in Agronomy* 89 (2006): 151–152.

Field Harvest Timing Below 15° Latitude

Close to the equator, harvests should occur as blossoming begins, then plants will re-grow. Since blossoming is more frequent at lower latitudes, harvests should also be more frequent. Each harvest will be smaller as well. With the exception of very high altitudes, stevia will grow as a perennial in these latitudes, with 4–6 harvests per year.

Closest to the equator, stevia blossoming may be nearly continuous, necessitating frequent harvests during the early stages of blossoming. With stevia field trials in Indonesia (about lat 7°S), harvests were made every 1–2 months (7 harvests per year), with a cutting height of 15–20 cm (6–8 in.) above ground level. Even with such frequent cuttings, about 25% of the plant population was blossoming at the time of each cutting.[37] Blossoming inhibits further leaf growth and glycoside production. This is why delaying harvest for a long time after the onset of substantial blossoming could reduce total annual leaf yield.

There appears to be some potential for selecting stevia genotypes with delayed blossoming under the year-round 12–13 hour natural photoperiod found close to the equator. In a Brazilian study, researchers were able to identify a few genotypes that exhibited minimal blossoming for a longer period of time at the 12-hour photoperiod as compared to other genotypes.[38]

---

[37] S. Basuki and Sumaryono, "Effect of black plastic mulch and plant density on the growth of weeds and stevia," *BIOTROP special publication 38*, 1990, 107–113.

[38] Zaidan, Dietrich, and Felippe, "Effect of photoperiod on flowering"

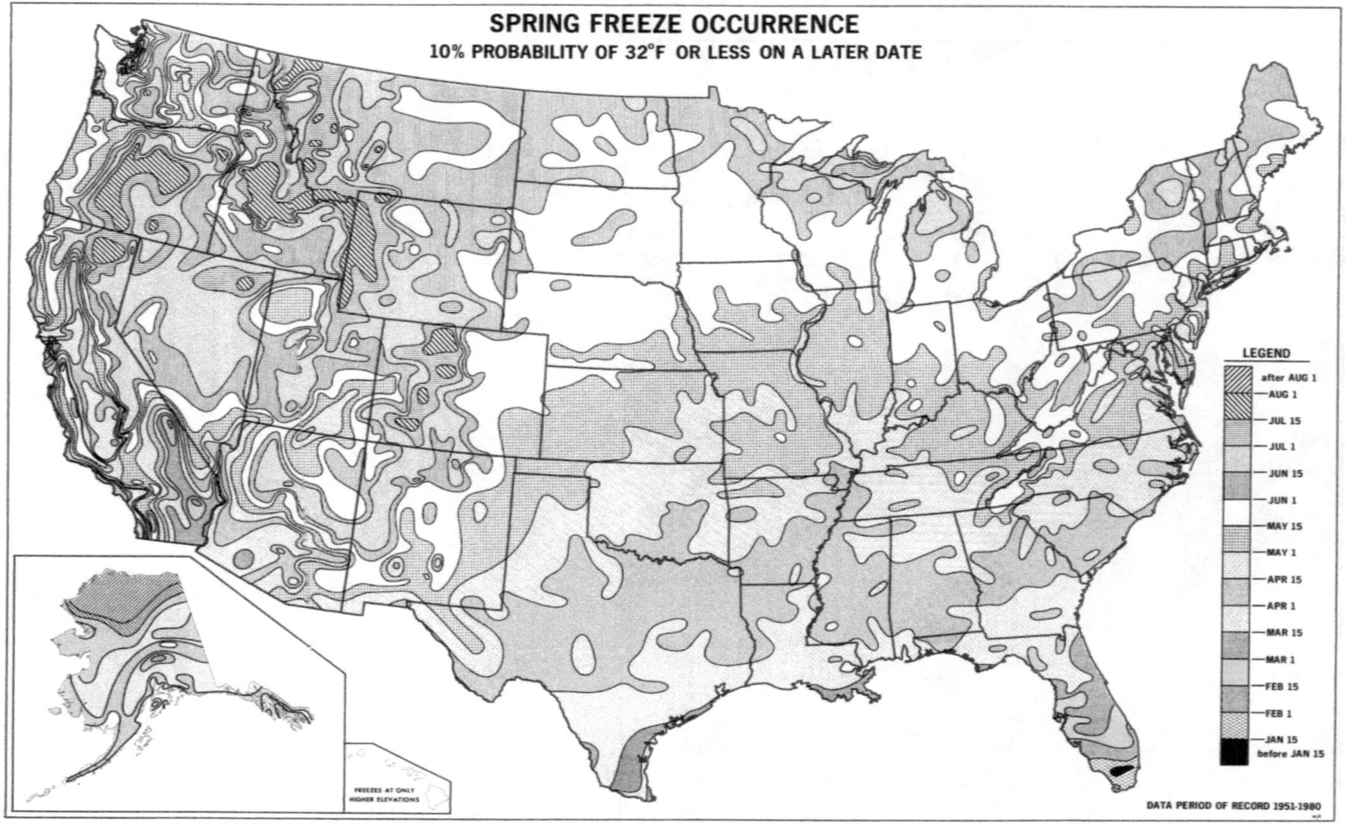

Figure 6: Last spring freeze dates in the U.S.A.
From the National Climatic Data Center, http://www.ncdc.noaa.gov/oa/climate/freezefrost/frostfreemaps.html

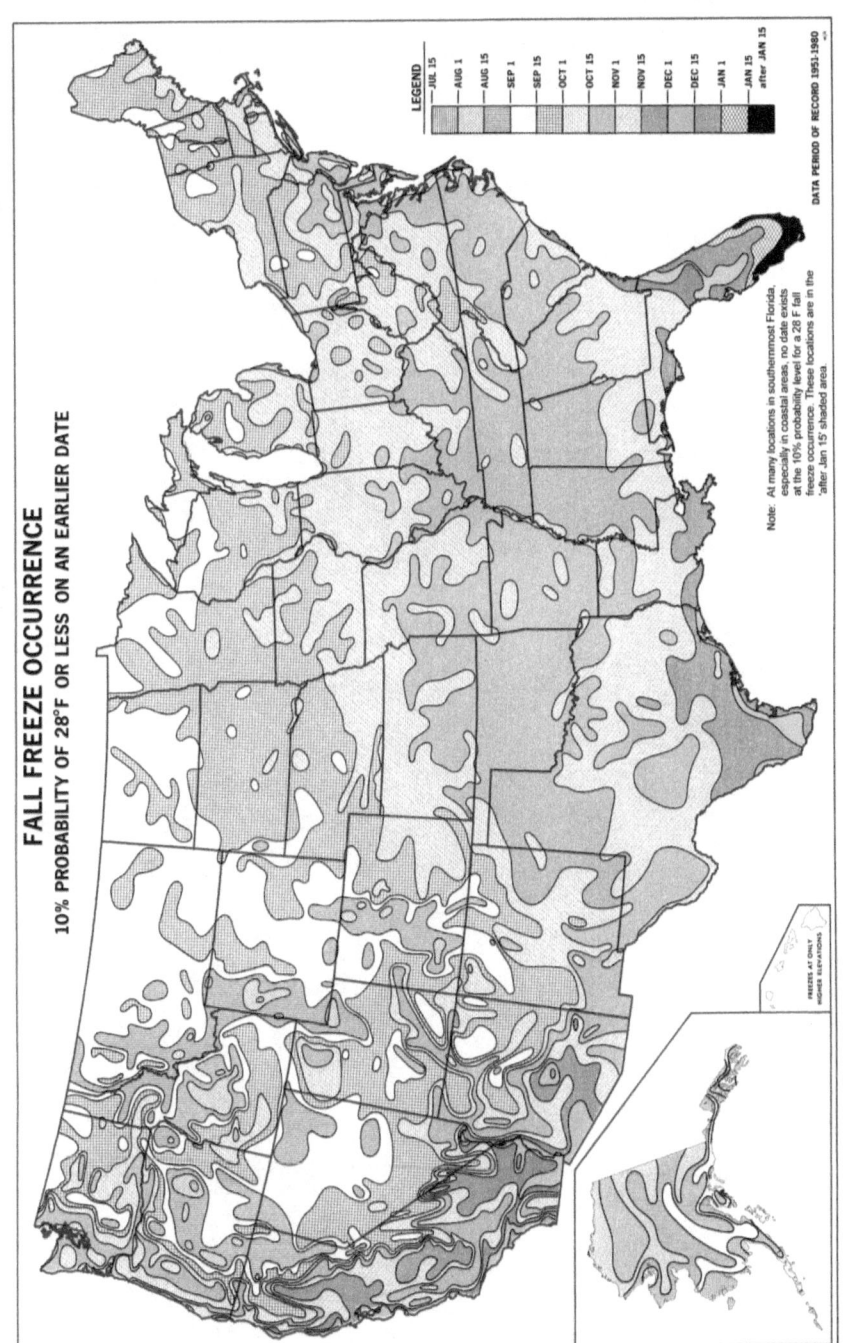

Figure 7: First fall freeze dates in the U.S.A.
From the National Climatic Data Center, http://www.ncdc.noaa.gov/oa/climate/freezefrost/frostfreemaps.html

Chapter 2

Plant Propagation

Stevia may be started from seed or by asexual methods such as stem cuttings, crown division, or tissue culture. Factors affecting the choice of propagation method include:

- customer requirements
- effect on yield
- effect on glycoside levels
- effect on diseases
- costs
- production cycle (annual or perennial)
- field size
- availability of expertise and labor

Choosing a Propagation Method

When labor costs are taken into consideration, starting stevia from seed is usually less expensive than using asexual methods. Therefore the decision often comes down to whether the advantages of asexual methods outweigh the extra cost. After initial establishment, mature plants can be used as mother plants for propagation by stem cuttings or crown division.

Meeting customer requirements

A particular wholesale customer may require or prefer a particular cultivar (genotype or genetic strain developed for cultivation). In that case, you may not have a choice in propagation method. Some cultivars are only available by asexual propagation (usually stem cuttings). This is because many genotypes are not capable of consistently producing viable seeds. Some wholesale leaf buyers have developed their own proprietary cultivars, available only to their own growers. Some will provide planting material to their growers and then buy back stevia leaves.

Genetics

Asexual propagation methods such as stem cuttings, tissue culture, or crown divisions will preserve the genetic characteristics of the parent plant. You are basically cloning a plant. On the other hand, sexual reproduction (from seed), results in greater genetic variability. Plants grown from seed will inherit characteristics from the parents, but some genetic variation will be found as well. This variation is useful in a breeding program, but can reduce the uniformity of a crop.

Glycoside content

Leaf glycoside content is a key factor for a stevia crop. In most stevia genotypes, stevioside is the main sweet glycoside.[39] Some processors extract a range of different glycosides, including stevioside. However, some stevia processors are

---

[39] Some writers use the term "stevioside" in reference to all the glycosides in stevia rebaudiana collectively. But properly speaking, stevioside is only one of the sweet glycosides in stevia.

concerned with maximizing Rebaudioside A (Reb-A) content. Glycoside composition and content is partially determined by genetics and partially by growth factors such as day length. Especially for the extraction of white stevia extract powder, it may be deemed important to maximize Reb-A content. This generally means using asexual propagation from parent plants known to be genetically disposed for high Reb-A production. However, companies are beginning to develop seed-grown cultivars that are supposed to produce consistently high Reb-A output. So far, these proprietary seed-grown cultivars have not been made available to the general public.[40]

There is at least one cultivar advertised as "high Reb-A" that is available to the general public. It is known as *Crazy Sweet*[tm] and is available as a plant, reproduced asexually. It is sold by Richters Herbs in Canada.

When producing stevia for use as whole leaf or green stevia powder, the precise glycoside composition is less important. I have tried several different *Stevia rebaudiana* genotypes (genetic lines). Some are better than others, but I have found all of them to have an acceptable taste for herbal tea and green stevia powder. Of course, I am always looking for stevia genotypes with better taste and other beneficial characteristics.

Within the same genotype, propagation method does not appear to affect stevioside yield. Trials in the Czech Republic revealed no difference in yield of stevioside per gram of dried leaf between plants propagated by stem cuttings or grown from seeds.[41] Neither was there found to be a difference in

---

[40] In 2009, GLG Life Tech Corp. issued press releases about their new stevia cultivars said to be high in Rebaudioside A and reproduced by seed. See http://www.glglifetech.com/Media_Center/Press_Releases.
Additional stevia-related companies are listed in the appendix.

[41] Nepovim et al., "The effect of cultivation conditions"

total stevioside content per plant. In the case of named varieties, choices are more limited when growing from seed. Some of the improved stevia varieties are not available from seed.

Diseases

Some diseases such as septoria may be passed along through vegetative (asexual) propagation, but not through seeds. Septoria leaf spot has been a significant problem in Canadian field production and elsewhere. Unfortunately, the fungicide sprays that work against septoria tend to leave high levels of residue and would not qualify for organic production.[42] The best solution for septoria is propagation from seed or selecting resistant strains for vegetative propagation. I do not know of resistant strains available to the public, but farmers can try selecting plants that seem unaffected and propagate those by stem cuttings.

Leaf yield

Of all the propagation methods, large crown divisions would be expected to produce the highest leaf yield in annual production or the first year of perennial production. Crown divisions result from dividing mature plants (at least a year old). A single plant is usually divided into three plants. The well established root systems give plants a fast start. Tissue culture and stem cuttings (the other asexual methods) should produce a slightly higher yield the first year as compared to seed-grown plants, but less than from crown divisions. The difference in yield would vary from year to year and depend on climate and soil type.

---

[42] Jim Brandle, "Stevia," in Rita Berzins, Helen Snell, and Conrad Richter, eds., *Richters Third Commercial Herb Growing Conference* (Goodwood, Ontario: Richters, 1999) 155–160.

A study in Egypt compared propagation from seed, crown divisions, and tissue culture.[43] Trials were undertaken at the Agricultural Research Center Experimental Station—Giza, Egypt (about lat 30°N). Crown divisions were taken from year-old plants, with three divisions from each plant. Plants from seed were transplanted to the field 75 days after sowing. For all treatments, five cuttings were taken during the first year of growth. Cuttings were taken at 90, 180, 240, 300, and 360 days from transplanting to the field. Crown divisions and tissue culture resulted in significantly higher dry leaf yields as compared to seed in all but the fifth cutting. For a one-year period (five cuttings), the dry leaf yields (averaged from two seasons and three fertilization treatments) were as follows:

- From seed:
  3.16 tonnes/feddan (7524 kg/ha, 6719 lb/acre)
- From tissue culture:
  3.89 tonnes/feddan (9262 kg/ha, 8271 lb/acre)
- From crown divisions:
  4.12 tonnes/feddan (9810 kg/ha, 8760 lb/acre)

---

[43] Attia et al., "Effect of Propagation Method and Nitrogen"

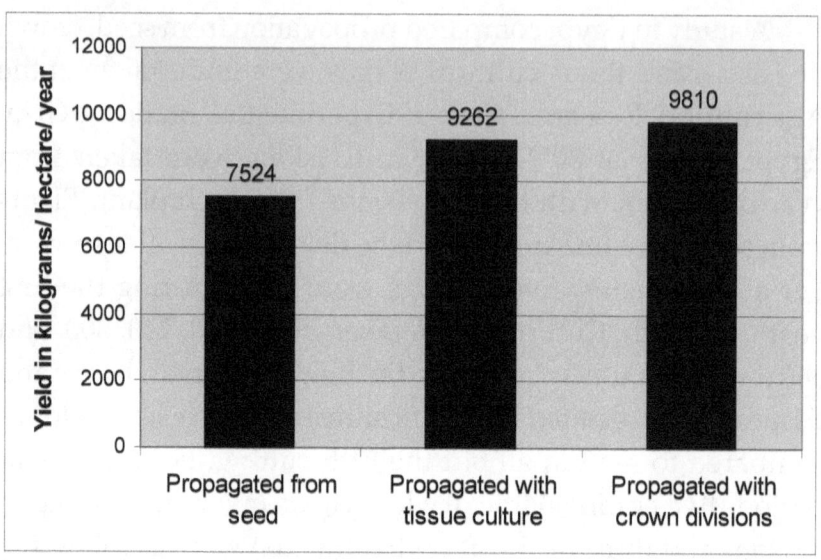

Figure 8: Dry leaf yield by propagation method.[44]
From first year trials in Egypt with five harvests per year. Data averaged from two seasons and three fertilization treatments.

Growing Media

Growing media (potting soils) for starting cuttings or seeds typically contain a mixture of peat, horticultural vermiculite and/or perlite, and sometimes compost. Organic media are available for certified organic production. Commercially available media have been perfected for various uses and conditions. Media vendors can help you choose the best one. Steve Marsden of Herbal Advantage[45] (a supplier of stevia plants), recommends the Premier Pro-Mix line of grow-

---

[44] Ibid.
[45] Visit Herbal Advantage Inc. online at www.herbaladvantage.com.

ing media.[46] For rooting stem cuttings, Marsden uses *PRO-MIX 'BX'/ MYCORISE® PRO*.[47]

Greenhouse trials in Brazil (lat 23°S) showed chicken manure is a suitable substitute for chemical fertilizers in a growing medium for starting stevia transplants.[48] Researchers used a composted dried laying hen manure mixed with sandy clay loam soil and lime.

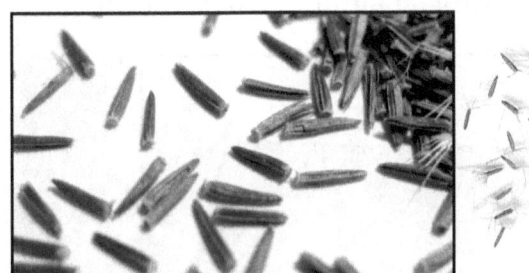 

Figure 9: Stevia seeds.

Starting Stevia from Seed

There was a time when stevia seeds were not a realistic option because they rarely achieved better than 50% germination. This is no longer the case. Good seeds with a high germination rate are now available. Be sure to get the *Stevia rebaudiana* species. Stevia seeds are very small, about the shape of lettuce or dandelion seeds. Small "pappus bristles"

---

[46] For information and to locate Premier Pro-Mix distributors, see: http://www.premierhort.com/eProMix/index.htm.

[47] See more about this growing medium at: http://www.premierhort.com/eProMix/Horticulture/Products/GrowingMediaCat/Biofungicide/fSubtilex.htm.

[48] J. W. P. Carneiro, A. S. Muniz, and T. A. Guedes, "Greenhouse bedding plant production of Stevia rebaudiana (Bert) Bertoni," *Canadian Journal of Plant Science* 77, no. 3 (1997): 473–474.

are attached to each seed. Most seed companies remove the pappus bristles for easier seed handling. Good seeds are black or dark in color.

If you have developed a good system for starting bedding plants from seed, go ahead and use it for stevia. After germination, be sure to expose plants to at least 15 hours of light per day to ensure good leaf growth without pre-mature blossoming. This usually means artificial lighting will be needed.

Figure 10: Nursery flat with cell-pack inserts.

For plants that will be transplanted to the field, plug production is commonly used. The simplest form of plug production uses plastic "nursery flats" with plastic inserts consisting of 72 "cells" in each flat. For small-scale production, two flats will fit under a standard fluorescent shop light. A clear plastic dome or cover can be used at first to maintain humidity and temperature. If a mechanical field transplanter will be used, the capabilities of the transplanter may dictate the type of plug system you will use.

It is probably best to use a commercial seed starting medium. These will typically contain a mixture of peat, horticultural vermiculite or perlite, fertilizer, and sometimes compost. Organic media are available for certified organic production. If the starting medium is dry, moisten it. Fill cells or pots level without compacting. Place one or two seeds in each cell or pot. Using two or more seeds will reduce the number of empty cells, but will require thinning. For a small number of flats, a vibrating hand seeder will be helpful. The battery operated Gro Mor™ hand seeder works well. Various automated seeders are also available for larger numbers of flats. A system that can sow lettuce seeds will probably work for stevia as long as pappus bristles are removed from seeds. Seeds should be sown on the surface or barely cover with fine horticultural vermiculite. Seeds will sprout a little better if light reaches them.[49]

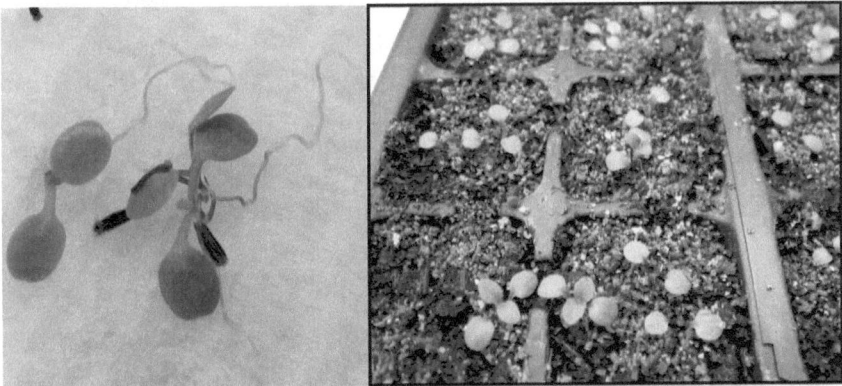

Figure 11: Newly sprouted stevia seedlings, 1–3 per cell.

Moisten gently to settle seeds. Be sure to keep seeds constantly moist as they sprout. Mist or gently sprinkle from

---

[49] Goettemoeller and Ching, "Seed Germination in Stevia rebaudiana"

above. Capillary watering systems are also available. These systems draw water up from below. During sprouting, some sort of clear cover is beneficial. Plant lights left on constantly for the first 2–3 weeks will aide germination and early growth. Standard fluorescent bulbs kept 5–12 in. (13–30 cm) above flats will do nicely. Keep the air temperature between 72°F (22°C) and 80°F (27°C). Temperature can be regulated in a growth chamber or by adjusting the height of the light or with a heat mat. The optimum temperature for stevia seed germination is about 77°F (25°C).[50]

In 6–12 days, tiny seedlings should begin to emerge. Remove the cover when more than half the pots or cells have seedlings showing. Don't leave it on too long as humid air will encourage damping off disease. At this point, leave the light on constantly at about 5–12 in. (13–30 cm) above plants. Keep the soil slightly moist, but not soggy.

Most commercial starting media contain enough fertilizer for optimum seedling growth. Seaweed fertilizer or other low-nitrogen fertilizer in the water starting at about the third watering may be helpful, but plants usually do well without added fertilizer. At about 2–3 weeks after sowing, begin to turn the light off at night. Maintain 15 hours of light per 24-hour period. A timer is nice for this job.

At about 7–10 weeks from sowing, plants may be transplanted to the field or left to grow a while longer. Young stevia seedlings tend to grow more slowly than other horticultural plants. Plants may also be transplanted to larger pots for

---

[50] Luciana Takahashi, Elena Melges E José Walter P. Carneiro, "Desempenho Germinativo De Sementes De Stevia rebaudiana Bertoni Sob Diferentes Temperaturas," [Germination Performance of Stevia Seeds Under Different Temperatures] *Brazilian Journal of Seeds* 18, no. 1, 1996: 1–5.

retail sales. Harden off plants for at least five days before transplanting to the field. Do this by gradually exposing plants to cooler temperatures and longer dry periods. Try not to expose plants to temperatures below 40°F, as this will slow their growth.

Figure 12: Young plants from seed in cell packs.

Figure 13: Growing stevia plants from stem cuttings.

Propagating Stevia from Stem Cuttings

During long-day conditions, stevia stems produce roots fairly easily. If you already have a system set up for propagating herbaceous plants from stem cuttings, it should work for stevia. Here I will describe the general principles involved.

You will need the following supplies:

- Mother plants, potted or in the field, from which to take cuttings.
- Fluorescent shop light or other plant light (in most cases).
- Coarse, well-draining growing medium designed for rooting cuttings.
- Small pots or cell packs with drainage holes.
- Clear cover for maintaining humidity (optional).
- Drip hose (if outdoors).
- Sharp knife or razor.

Stems root easily when two key conditions are met. First, at least 14 hours of fluorescent or natural light per day encourages quick rooting. Secondly, the rooting medium should be suited for rooting stem cuttings. These media are available commercially (see appendix) and typically contain a high percentage of coarse horticultural vermiculite, perlite, or another coarse potting material along with peat. Media suppliers can help you choose the best medium. Steve Marsden of Herbal Advantage recommends the Premier Pro-Mix line of growing media.[51] For the rooting of stem cuttings, Steve uses the *PRO-MIX 'BX'/ MYCORISE® PRO*. Use pots or cell packs with drainage holes in the bottom.

---

[51] For information and to locate Premier Pro-Mix distributors, see: http://www.premierhort.com/eProMix/index.htm.

Figure 14: Plants from stem cuttings. *Grown by Steve Marsden of Herbal Advantage Inc. (www.herbaladvantage.com).*

Use a sharp knife or razor to make a clean, slanting cut between leaf nodes. One long shoot can be sliced into several smaller stem cuttings, although trials in California indicated plants grown from tip cuttings grew faster and bigger.[52] Trials in Japan found first-year dry leaf yields were significantly higher when cuttings were taking from stem tips.[53]

Each cutting should be 4–6 in. (10–15 cm) in length. Trials in India found significantly better rooting with 15 cm (6 in.) cuttings compared to 7.5 cm (3 in.) cuttings.[54] Remove larger leaves. I do not usually treat cuttings before planting, but a study found pre-treatment with paclobutrazol at 50 or 100 ppm improved the induction of roots and sprouts from stevia stem cuttings.[55]

Gently insert cuttings into the growing medium with the end that was closer to the base of the plant pointed downward. The end that was further from the base should be pointed upward. At least two leaf buds should remain above ground level. Leaf buds are at the axis where older leaves attach to the stem. Lower leaf buds, with older leaves cut off, may be buried.

Periodic misting or a clear covering will be needed until the stems strike root. Mist or sprinkle every few hours when the sun is shining or temperatures are high. After 2–4 weeks, cuttings should develop roots, possibly poking out from the

---

[52] Shock, "Experimental Cultivation of Rebaudi's Stevia"

[53] 村山, 盛一; 茅野, 良一; 宮里, 清松; 野瀬, 昭博; Murayama, Seiichi; Kayano, Ryoichi; Miyazato, Kiyomatsu; Nose, Akihiro, テビアの栽培に関する研究: 第2 報施肥量・栽植密度・挿穂部位および苗の栄養系が生育と収量に及ぼす影響(農学科); ["Studies on the cultivation of Stevia rebaudiana BERTONI : II. Effects of the amount of fertilizer, planting density, position of the cutting and the seedling clone on growth and yield (Department of Agriculture)"] *The Science Bulletin of the Faculty of Agriculture. University of the Ryukyus* no. 27 (1980): 1–8.

[54] M. V. Chalapathi, S. Thimmegowda, N. D. Kumar, G. G. E. Rao, and K. Mallikarjuna, "Influence of length of cutting and growth regulators on vegetative propagation of Stevia (Stevia rebaudiana Bert.)," *Crop Research -HISAR.* 21 (2001): 53–56.

[55] Ibid.

drainage holes. Throw out any cuttings that wither and die or fail to produce roots. Successful cuttings may be transplanted to larger pots for retail plant sales or allow to grow another 2–4 weeks before transplanting outdoors.

Researcher Clinton Shock successfully rooted stem cuttings in a mist chamber. Plants were left in the chamber four weeks at 70°F (21°C) with 10 seconds of mist every 10 minutes.[56] Cuttings taken from stem tips rooted most quickly. Three-inch long cuttings were rooted in a mixture of peat, sand, and fertilizer on two by two inch spacing. Each cubic yard of mixed sand and peat was fertilized with the following mixture:

- 7.5 lb dolomitic lime
- 2.5 lb hydrated lime
- 2.5 lb single superphosphate
- 1.5 lb urea
- 3/8 lb of potassium sulfate
- ¼ lb of 12-12-12

Researchers at the University of Bonn, Germany (lat 50.6°N) conducted stevia stem cutting trials.[57] In the autumn of 2004, select mother plants were dug from the field and potted in 2.8-liter containers with a 1:1 mixture of sand and propagation substrate as the growing medium. These mother plants were kept in a vegetative state over the winter by exposure to light from grow lamps 16 hours per day. About 1500 propagated plants were obtained by rooting stem cuttings from 20

---

[56] Shock, "Experimental Cultivation of Rebaudi's Stevia"

[57] Christa Lankes and R. Pude, "Possibilities for Growth of European Stevia in Temperate Zones," in Jan M.C. Geuns, ed. *Proceedings of the 2nd Stevia Symposium 2008* (Leuven, Belgium: Euprint ed., 2008) 103–115.

mother plants. A better field survival rate (95%) and leaf yield was obtained by rooting in Jiffy pots™ as compared to compressed soil blocks.

Timing for rooting cuttings

For the sake of optimum rooting and fastest growth, the best time of year for starting stem cuttings is when natural day length is over 13 hours and getting longer in the spring. This is typically too late for optimum yields in annual production, but is an option for perennial production or where plants are needed for wintering over in colder climates. Wintered-over plants may be used as mother plants for winter stem cuttings.

Stem cuttings may be rooted outdoors under a shade cloth or lathe house when soil and air temperatures are expected to remain warm and day lengths are at least 13 hours and lengthening. At this time of year, stems for cuttings may be taken directly from selected plants in the field. Very close to the equator, days never get much longer than 12 hours. In this case, supplemental artificial lighting will be beneficial for preconditioning mother plants and for rooting the cuttings. Cuttings may be rooted in cell packs, pots, or directly in growing beds alongside a drip hose.

For the drip hose method, gently insert cuttings into the ground near a drip hose where the soil is constantly moist. It may help to poke a small hole in the ground, and then insert the cutting in that hole. Cuttings from mature mother plants will likely do better than those from younger plants.

Figure 15: Potted plants under fluorescent light in winter.

Pre-conditioning mother plants

For winter cuttings in cold climates, mother plants will be needed. These could be dug from the field in the fall and kept in a greenhouse or indoors under artificial light. Select the best plants and use pots at least one gallon in size. Some crowding of roots will be unavoidable. Large plants may be divided into two or three plants (see "Propagating Stevia with Crown Divisions" below). In order to avoid blossoming, use fluorescent or other plant lights to make sure potted plants always receive about 15 hours of light each day. Plants may survive the winter in a greenhouse without supplemental lighting, but results will be less consistent.

When stems are harvested for rooting, it should be from plants that have been exposed to a long photoperiod (14–16 hours per day) for at least 3 weeks. This pre-conditions plants for vegetative growth rather than blossoming. When there is insufficient natural light, this pre-conditioning must be done with fluorescent lighting or another type of plant light. The lights should be left on continuously for 15 hours during every 24-hour period. This should continue for at least three weeks prior to taking stem cuttings from the mother plants.

In some cases, you may wish to hold over stevia plants for replanting in the field the following year. Spring or summer cuttings could then be taken when days are naturally long. In this case, supplemental winter lighting for potted plants would not be as important, but still beneficial for better plant survival.

Figure 16: Stevia plant crowns being put into cold storage.

Cold storage of stevia roots

Another possibility for overwintering mother plants is cold storage of roots. This involves overwintering plant roots in a dormant state in a cold cellar or basement. The technique is similar to that used in storing root crops.

With tops already harvested, dig roots and pack in a bucket or other container surrounded by moist soil, potting soil, sand, or similar medium. Place these containers in a dark place where the temperature remains above freezing and below about 55°F (12°C). Cover the bucket with something like straw or burlap to hold in moisture while allowing some exchange of air.

The plants may be replanted back into the field after the soil warms and after your average last frost date. If roots are large, they may be divided into two or three plants (crown division) before replanting.

Figure 17: Multi-stem stevia plant that could be divided.

Propagating Stevia with Crown Divisions

The crown of a plant is where shoots emerge from the root system. Over time, a stevia plant sends up new shoots from the crown and the plant gradually expands in size. Crown division is done by digging up an entire plant, dividing it into two or more plants, and replanting those now smaller plants. Some of the root system and one or more above-ground stems go with each new plant. Typically, you might get three divisions from a plant that is at least a year old. Plant tops should normally be harvested before divisions are made.

Propagation by crown division might be impractical for large fields because of the labor requirement. Divisions are made by hand with the help of a trowel or spade. Also, the hole dug for transplanting into the field must be large enough to accommodate the root system of each division. But if labor is available, crown division can be a way to expand production. Usually, early growth will be more rapid than with other propagation methods because the root system is already well developed.

Propagation by crown division is well suited to a perennial production cycle because the work involved will be rewarded by multiple years of production. Also, division may be used to renew older plants, as with rhubarb or irises. After 3–5 years of perennial production, yield tends to decline. At that time, plants may be dug up and divided if they are still disease-free. Those plants will be renewed and production area will be expanded.

Crown division can be useful in other situations as well, even where annual field production is necessary. If you keep mother plants in a greenhouse for propagation from cuttings, they may be renewed and multiplied periodically by dividing crowns and repotting in new pots, with new potting soil. Also, crown division may be useful for plants dug from the field at the end of the growing season to be wintered over indoors. If plants have grown too large for your selected pots, they may be divided into smaller plants.

Breeding Through Selection

Because of natural genetic variation, some plants in a group of seed-grown plants will have genetic characteristics better suited to your local conditions. These genetically superior plants may be propagated by cuttings, crown division, or tissue culture. These asexual propagation methods will almost completely preserve the genetic makeup of a plant from one generation to the next. Asexually reproduced plants are clones of the mother plant.

Starting with a field of seed-grown plants, you may discover some plants that blossom later, grow better, yield better, taste better, or resist troublesome diseases. This requires close observation and careful record keeping. Look for the characteristic or combination of characteristics you are trying to improve upon. This is not an exact science, because some differences in a given year may be affected by climatic and other factors in addition to genetics.

For accurate yield trials, dry the leaves thoroughly, then weigh and compare. The yield from a single plant is not going to be a decisive factor, but it can be considered in combination with other observations. After an individual plant is asexually propagated, the new plants can be grown out. The average yield from these offspring will have more meaning for the purposes of comparison because of the larger sample size.

In a cold-winter climate, dig selected mother plants and bring them indoors for the winter. This can be done by potting the plants and keeping them under fluorescent lights or other plant lights through the winter (see instructions above). This will make early spring cuttings possible. Another option is to keep dormant roots in cold storage through the winter (see instructions above).

Chapter 3

Field Preparation and Plant Care

In general, ideal agronomic practices for stevia are similar to those for transplanted vegetable crops or other horticultural crops. Conditions suitable for vegetable crops will probably be suitable for stevia, though fertilization requirements are lower than for most vegetable crops.

Field Location

Stevia prefers full or partial sun exposure. If your summers are very hot, afternoon shade might be beneficial. If your summers are cool and cloudy, allow as much sun exposure as possible. Avoid locations susceptible to standing water and poor drainage. Stevia prefers moist, but not saturated soils. Raised beds or ridge tillage may be beneficial where soils are high in clay or poorly draining.

Soils and Fertilization

Stevia grows well on a wide range of soil types. The ideal soil would be a sandy loam or loam, high in organic matter. Stevia thrives with a wide range of soil pH levels, from acid to moderately alkaline. A source from India indicates an ideal pH range of 5–7.5 for stevia.[58] In Egypt, good stevia leaf yields were obtained with a soil pH of 8.1.[59]

A test of soil samples can help determine what might be missing. The laboratory analysis of soil samples may include fertilization recommendations. Soil fertility requirements for stevia are similar to those for vegetable crops, although stevia has a fairly low nitrogen requirement. Compost, aged manure, or other organic soil amendments can be good slow-release sources of nitrogen and other nutrients. Slow release is beneficial for steady leaf growth without producing the weak plant tissues that can occur from excessive nitrogen availability. Organic matter in aged manure and compost can also improve the water holding capacity of the soil and nourish beneficial soil organisms.

Small-scale field trials in Germany during the year 2003 demonstrated the advantage of stable manure over other fertilizers tried (see fig. 18). This was an unusually hot, dry year. All fertilizer application treatments except stable manure resulted in lower dry leaf yields as compared to the control (no added fertilizer).[60] Stable manure produced a higher dry leaf/flower yield (4420 kg/ha or 3947 lb/acre) as compared to the control (4170 kg/ha or 3724 lb/acre). Annual stevioside and

---

[58] Singh and Rao, "Stevia: The Herbal Sugar"
[59] Attia et al., "Effect of Propagation Method and Nitrogen"
[60] Pude, Schmitz-Eiberger, and Noga, "Development, Yield"

Rebaudioside A yield was also highest with stable manure. Treatments were as follows:

- No fertilizer applied (control)
- Calcium ammonium nitrate (KAS) (27% N; at 370 kg/ha).
- Stable manure (3% N, 4% phosphorous, 6% potassium; at 3330 kg/ha or 2974 lb/acre).
- Agrobiosol (7% N, 2% phosphorous, 3% potassium; at 420 kg/ha)
- Potassium magnesia (KMg) (30% potassium, 10% magnesium; at 560 kg/ha)
- KAS + KMg (27% N, 30% phosphorous, 10% magnesium; at 3.7 dt/ha KAS and 560 kg/ha KMg).

Preliminary results from trials in 2004 confirmed the advantage of stable manure for stevia fertilization.

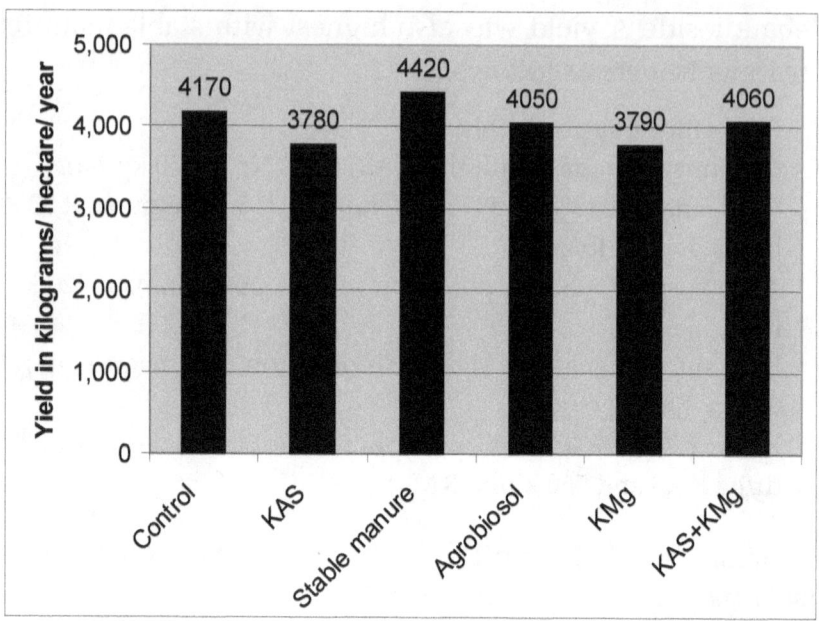

Figure 18: Dry leaf yield by fertilization treatment.[61] *Yields extrapolated from small-scale field trials in 2003 with an annual production cycle near Bonn, Germany (lat 50.6°N).*

Organic amendments such as aged manure or compost can be mixed into soil during plowing, spading, rotary tilling, or discing. With some drip irrigation systems, nitrogen and other fertilizers can also be injected into the irrigation water during the growing season.

A study in Egypt compared different nitrogen fertilization application levels for perennial stevia production. Small-scale field trials were undertaken at the Agricultural Research Center Experimental Station—Giza, Egypt (about lat 30°N).[62] Plants were grown on a silt clay loam soil with the following properties:

---

[61] Ibid.
[62] Attia et al., "Effect of Propagation Method and Nitrogen"

- 12.16% sand, 48.85% silt, and 38.99% clay
- pH of 8.10
- Available: 11.00 ppm N, 9.12 ppm P, and 35.86 ppm K
- E.C. (mmohs/m3): 2.65
- CaCO3: 1.81%

Field transplanting was done on April 1. Five cuttings were taken per year, at 90, 180, 240, 300, and 360 days from transplanting to the field.

Application of urea fertilizer (46.5% nitrogen) at 40 kg/feddan/cutting (95 kg/ha/cutting or 85 lb/acre/cutting) produced the highest yield. The first application of 40 kg/feddan was done at the beginning of the growing season in two doses, before the first and second irrigations. After each cutting, the application was again made in two doses before irrigations. For a one year period (five cuttings), total dry leaf yield (averaged from two seasons and three propagation treatments) was as follows:

- With no nitrogen fertilizer applied:
  3.53 tonnes/feddan (8405 kg/ha or 7497 lb/acre)
- With 20 kg N/feddan/cutting (48 kg/ha or 42 lb/acre/cutting):
  3.73 tonnes/feddan (8881 kg/ha or 7927 lb/acre)
- With 40 kg N/feddan/cutting (95 kg/ha or 85 lb/acre/cutting):
  3.91 tonnes/feddan (9310 kg/ha or 8304 lb/acre)

As illustrated in figure 19, the yield increase resulting from nitrogen fertilization was small.

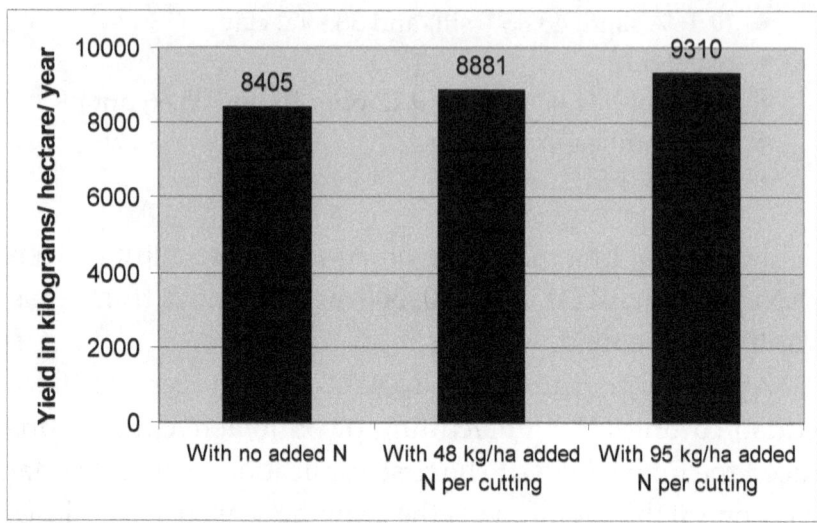

Figure 19: Dry leaf yield by nitrogen fertilization level.[63]
Extrapolated from first year small-scale field trials in Egypt with five cuttings per year. Data averaged from two seasons and three propagation treatments.

For annual field production in southern Ontario, Canada, researchers recommended 100 kg/ha (89 lb/acre) of 6-24-24 just before planting and 140 kg/ha (125 lb/acre) of urea in split applications.[64] The soils in southern Ontario are typically sandy, subject to leaching losses of nitrogen.

In a location with a tropical climate (Bangalore, India, lat 13°N), small-scale field trials showed significantly improved yield from a single application of NPK (nitrogen, phosphorous, and potassium) by incorporation into the soil.[65] Results

---

[63] Ibid.

[64] Mike Columbus, "The Cultivation of Stevia, Nature's Sweetener," OMAFRA Herb Series, 1997.
http://www.omafra.gov.on.ca/english/crops/facts/stevia.htm.

[65] M. V. Chalapathi, B. Shivaraj, and V. R. Ramakrishana, "Nutrient uptake and yield of Stevia (Stevia rebaudiana Bertoni) as influenced by methods of planting and fertilizer levels," *Crop Research -HISAR* 14, no. 2 (1997): 205–208.

are illustrated in figure 20. The soil type was an alfisol, with a pH of 6.5 and medium availability of N, P, and K. Yield results are from a single harvest, 100 days after transplanting to the field.

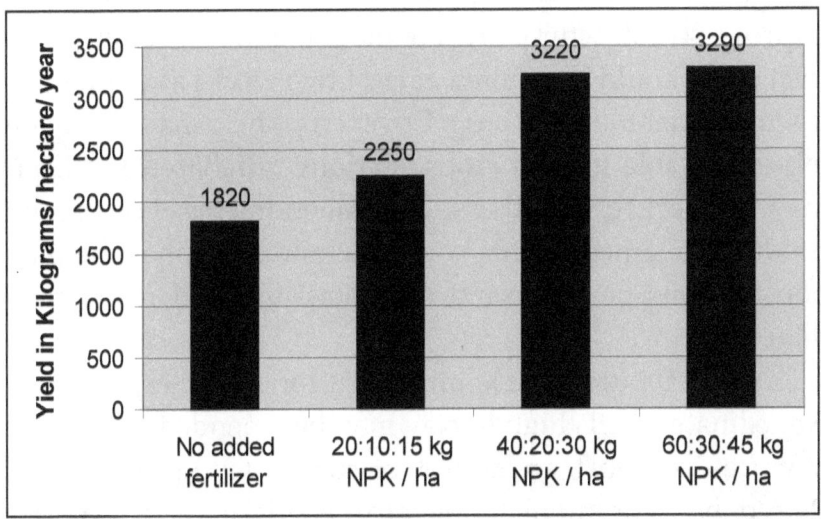

Figure 20: Dry leaf yield by fertilization level in India.[66]
From a single harvest 100 days after transplanting to the field in Bangalore, India. Single application of fertilizer by incorporation into the soil.

Researchers in Karnataka, India (about lat 15°N, tropical monsoon climate) investigated the use of "biofertilizers" in combination with farmyard manure for fertilizing stevia. Biofertilizers are meant to enhance soil life and help plants make better use of soil nutrients. The best yield was obtained with a combination of PSB (phosphorus solubilizing bacteria), VAM (vesicular arbuscular mycorrhiza), and AZO (Azospiril-

---

[66] Ibid.

lum). This combination produced a 12.84% improvement in fresh biomass yield over farmyard manure alone.[67]

A cover crop (or "green manure") can also enhance soil fertility.[68] For instance, a mixture of peas (a nitrogen-fixing legume) and oats could be planted in the fall. Roots and tops improve soil structure, organic matter, and soil fertility. The cash crop should be planted at least two weeks after tilling or discing under the cover crop. Cover crops help make nutrients more available to cash crops. Various purchased fertilizers may be worked into the soil as amendments. For organic production, amendments could include rock phosphate for phosphorous or greensand for potassium and many trace minerals.

Adequate drainage is important for stevia, especially in wet climates. Soils high in clay may be amended with green manures, compost, greensand, or composted farm manures. Raised beds or ridge tilling are beneficial for preventing standing water around plants on heavy soils or in low-lying areas. Green manure crops and compost would also be beneficial for sandy, sandy loam, and loam soils. For these soils, you could choose from raised beds, ridge tilling, or conventional flat tillage row cropping systems.

---

[67] Kuntal Das, Raman Dang, and T. N. Shivananda, "Effect of biofertilizers on the nutrient availability in soil in relation to growth, yield and yield attributes of Stevia rebaudiana," *Archives of Agronomy and Soil Science* 55, no. 4 (2009): 359–366.

[68] For more about cover crops or green manure, see Preston Sullivan, "Overview of Cover Crops and Green Manures," ATTRA – National Sustainable Agriculture Information Service, ATTRA Publication #IP024, 2003. http://attra.ncat.org/attra-pub/covercrop.html.

Finally, reports have been made that foliar sprays of micronutrients like boron and manganese can significantly increase stevia dry leaf yield and stevioside content.[69]

Field Tillage

Initial field tillage can be done as you would for vegetable crops. When done by machinery, this might involve harrowing and plowing followed by discing, rotary tilling, or rotary spading. A weed-free field is important because of stevia's susceptibility to weed pressure and the difficulty of weed control, especially when mulch will not be used.

Figure 21: Small raised growing beds.

In a raised bed planting system, the final tillage operation is done with a bed shaping implement or by hand. Some bed shapers will also install mulch films and drip irrigation lines. When beds are made by a tractor-drawn bed shaper, tractor

---

[69] See Azhar Ali Farooqi, and B. S. Sreeramu, *Cultivation of medicinal and aromatic crops* (Hyderabad: Universities Press, 2001) 635.

tires will run in paths between beds. Bed width would be determined by tractor tire spacing and the capabilities of the bed shaper. If you intend to use mulch films or plastic tunnel row covers, available widths of these materials must be taken into consideration as well. When field work is to be done by hand, bed width might be determined by accessibility from paths. Typically, a 3–5 ft. (91–152 cm) wide bed will permit easy access.

With loam or heavy clay soils, raised beds or ridges are likely to give better results as compared to a flat field. A study in India found slightly better yields from a ridge and furrow system (2700 kg/ha or 2411 lb/acre) as compared to raised beds with flat tops (2590 kg/ha or 2313 lb/acre).[70] With ridge and furrow, a single row is planted atop a narrow ridge.

For large-scale mechanized production, Steve Marsden of Herbal Advantage (US) recommends a traditional flat, single-row system with plants spaced 12–18 in. (30.5–45.7 cm) apart in the row and rows spaced for equipment or about 14–30 in. (35.6–76.2 cm) apart.[71] This layout accommodates tillage and cultivation implements commonly available in row-cropping regions, reducing equipment costs. The single-row system was used for stevia field trials in Kansas (US). Plants were spaced one foot apart in the row and rows were spaced two feet apart.[72]

---

[70] Chalapathi, Shivaraj, and Ramakrishana. "Nutrient uptake and yield of Stevia"
[71] Steve Marsden, personal correspondence, 2009.
[72] Janke, *Farming a Few Acres of Herbs: Stevia*

Figure 22: Stevia in raised beds with overhead irrigation.
Photos provided by Sunfruits Ltd. in India. Used with permission. http://www.sunfruit.biz/.

Irrigation

In general, stevia prefers consistent moisture, but dislikes saturated soils or standing water. Irrigation is essential for a successful stevia crop in most regions. Even where total annual rainfall is adequate, dry spells can reduce yields.

Stevia roots grow close to the soil surface and a consistent moisture supply is important. Therefore irrigation should be frequent and light. During periods without rainfall, watering should be done at least once per week, or when stem tips begin to droop. During periods of extreme heat and sunshine, stem tips may droop during the day even when soil moisture is adequate. Instruments such as tensiometers may be used to measure soil moisture levels for help in irrigation timing. Any type of mulch will tend to decrease evaporation from the soil and increase the intervals between watering.

Consistent rainfall throughout the growing season is rare. Irrigation will likely increase profits by boosting yields. In the year 2001, Kansas State University researchers grew stevia with irrigation near Wichita, Kansas and non-irrigated near Hayes, Kansas (US).[73] The non-irrigated site yielded about half the dry leaf weight (32 g/plant) of the irrigated site (72 g/plant). Both sites used an annual production cycle. Wichita (lat 37.6°N) is in USDA Plant Hardiness Zone 6a, while Hayes (lat 38.9°N) is in zone 5b. Average annual precipitation is about 32 in. (81.3 cm) at Wichita and 23 in. (58.4 cm) at Hayes.[74]

If a system for furrow irrigation, flood irrigation, or overhead irrigation is already in place, these may be used for

---

[73] Janke, *Farming a Few Acres of Herbs: Stevia*
[74] Data from U.S. Department of Agriculture, based on years 1971–2000.

irrigating stevia. Some sort of drip irrigation is probably the best choice, however. By delivering water directly to the root zone, drip irrigation avoids wetting leaves. Wet leaves can encourage disease. Drip irrigation also uses less water than overhead or flood irrigation and works well with plastic or paper mulches. In fact, drip irrigation is necessary with non-permeable mulches. Drip lines are laid down prior to transplanting, usually at the same time as the mulch. Drip lines may be laid by hand or machine.

Drip irrigation requires a clean water supply to avoid clogging. Filters are usually part of the system. Local extension agents or vendors of irrigation systems may be able to help you design the best system and layout for your conditions. For instance, drip lines should be spaced closer together for sandy soils than for heavier clay soils. On a small scale, a simple drip irrigation system may be designed with recycled rubber "weeping" drip hoses. These are attached to a regular garden hose.

Organic or plastic mulch will reduce evaporative water loss. This should result in lower irrigation costs. Trials in Slovakia showed that mulching with plastic sheets helped stevia plants go longer before experiencing stress from lack of moisture.[75]

---

[75] Katarína ČERNÁ, "Physiological changes in Stevia rebaudiana (Bertoni) leaves caused by root sphere conditions," *Journal of Central European Agriculture* 2, no. 1-2 (2001).

Figure 23: Stevia plant with rubber drip hose. *In a raised bed with straw mulch. A drip hose is usually placed underneath the mulch.*

Mulching

Mulch can boost profits in many cases. In the case of plastic mulch, benefits can include reduced weed growth, soil warming, conservation of soil moisture, reduced fertilizer leaching, increased nutrient availability, and reduced soil erosion.[76] Organic mulches can reduce weed growth, reduce soil erosion, cool soil, conserve moisture, and improve soil fertility. Organic mulches can include straw, hay, shredded leaves, or various types of compost. Manufactured sheet or

---

[76] See V.A. Clarkson, "Effect of Black Polyethylene mulch on soil and microclimate temperature and nitrate level," *Agron. J.* 52 (1960): 307–309.

film mulches can include permeable or impermeable plastics and paper-based products of various colors.

Paper or plastic sheet/film mulches are usually applied before transplanting. Where summers are hot and a sheet-type mulch is not used, a few inches of an organic mulch such as weed-free hay, straw or shredded leaves may be beneficial. This should be applied after the soil and air temperatures are steadily warm.

Mechanized implements are available for organic mulch application on a large scale. Plastic or paper-based films are also suitable for mechanized application and removal. Tractor-drawn implements are available that can form beds, lay down drip irrigation lines, and install mulch. Mulches may also be laid by hand. For the transplanting operation, holes are punched through the mulch by hand or with a tractor-drawn transplanter.

Standard plastic is not biodegradable and must be disposed of in a landfill after use. However, biodegradable paper and plastic film alternatives are now available. These may be suitable for an annual production cycle or the first year of a perennial cycle. They are designed to break down after a single growing season. Trials conducted by Washington State University found biodegradable mulches performed as well as standard black plastic for a basil crop.[77]

Costs and benefits

Based on available studies, mulching looks promising. Not only does it tend to boost yields, but it can also reduce the cost of labor for weed control.

---

[77] Carol Miles, Lydia Garth, Madhu Sonde, and Martin Nicholson, "Searching for Alternatives to Plastic Mulch," Washington State Uuniversity Vancouver Research and Extension Unit, 2004.

Small-scale field trials at Sukabumi, West Java, Indonesia (tropical, about lat 7°S) evaluated the use of black plastic mulch and various planting densities for stevia.[78] The experiment lasted a year. The soil was andosol sandy loam with 5% organic matter. Black polyethylene plastic sheet mulch was used (0.08 mm thickness) with 2.5 cm (1 in.) diameter holes for plants. Seven harvests were taken during that time. Shoots were cut 15–20 cm (6–8 in.) above ground level every 1–2 months. About 25% of plants were blossoming at harvest time. Yield totals are illustrated in figure 24. Yields were significantly better with black plastic mulch at all planting densities versus the control. With a planting density of 500 plants/24 m^2 (about 20.8/m^2, 208,000/ha, or 84,211/acre), approximate yields were as follows:

Yield using black plastic mulch:
About 1.38 kg/m^2 (13,800 kg/ha or 12,323 lb/acre)

Yield without using any mulch:
About 1.04 kg/m^2 (10,400 kg/ha or 9287 lb/acre)

These results indicate a more than 25% yield increase using plastic mulch versus no mulch at the highest planting density.

---

[78] Basuki and Sumaryono, "Effect of black plastic mulch and plant density"

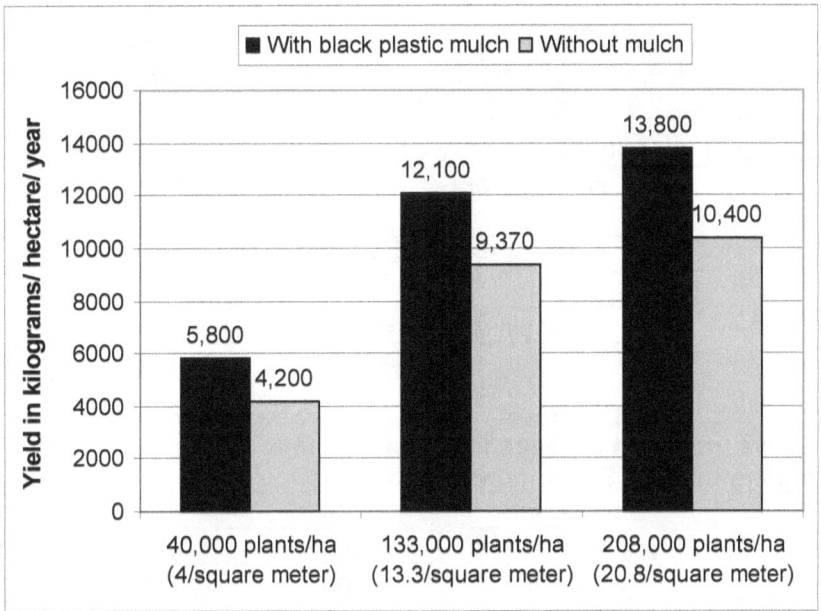

Figure 24: Approximate dry leaf yield with black plastic mulch versus no mulch.[79] *Yield in one year extrapolated from small-scale field trials with perennial production cycle near Sukabumi, West Java, Indonesia (about lat 7°S).*

Figure 25 lists the dried leaf yield increase from using black plastic mulch versus no mulch in the Indonesian study. Figure 25 also shows the gross income increase from using black plastic mulch assuming dried leaf is sold at US $2 per pound. Even at this conservative price per pound, the potential gross income advantage is considerable under the conditions of the study.

---

[79] Data from Basuki and Sumaryono, "Effect of black plastic mulch and plant density"

Plants per square meter:	4	13.3	20.8
Plants per hectare:	40,000	133,000	208,000
Plants per acre:	16,194	53,846	84,211
First year yield differences from using plastic mulch vs. no mulch			
per hectare:	+1600 kg	+2730 kg	+3400 kg
per acre:	+1427 lbs	+2435 lbs	+3033 lbs
per plant:	+40 grams	+21 grams	+16 grams
	+1.41 oz	+0.74 oz	+0.56 oz
Gross income difference from using plastic mulch (assuming USD $2 per pound for dry leaf)			
per hectare:	+$7027	+$12,029	+$14,983
per acre:	+$2845	+$4870	+$6066
per plant:	+$0.17	+$0.09	+$0.07

Figure 25: Appoximate dry leaf yield and gross income difference using black plastic mulch. [80] *As compared to mulch-free. Based on yield in first year from small-scale field trials with perennial production cycle near Sukabumi, West Java, Indonesia (about lat 7°S).*

Stevia production trials in the south of Slovakia (about lat 48°N) compared the use of white PVC sheet mulch, black PVC sheet mulch, and a control with no mulch.[81] The highest yield of dried stevia leaves resulted from use of the white PVC sheet mulch. Mulching also allowed the plants to persist longer before a lack of moisture brought about plant stress or death. The average high and low temperatures in the warmest month (July) are 80°F and 56°F (26.7°C and 13.3°C) for this part of

---

[80] Data from Basuki and Sumaryono, "Effect of black plastic mulch and plant density."
[81] ČERNÁ, "Physiological changes in Stevia"

Slovakia. The average high and low temperatures in the coldest month are 34°F and 23°F (1.1°C and −5°C).[82]

A study at Kiev (Kyiv), Ukraine (about lat 50°N) found that mulching with black plastic increased dry leaf yield by 2670 kg/ha/year (2384 lb/acre) as compared to the control (no mulch).[83] The planting density was 80,000 plants/ha. With black plastic mulch, the total yield was 5430 kg/ha/year (4849 lb/acre).

Both plastic and organic mulches will reduce evaporation from the soil surface. A study in the western desert of Egypt found a 50% water savings from using plastic mulch on grape vineyards rather than hoeing or herbicides for weed control.[84] Straw mulch saved water as well.

Weed control is a major benefit of mulching with plastic or paper sheets. Assuming no yield difference, a cost benefit analysis could involve comparing the cost of using mulch against the cost of other methods of weed control. Mulch will greatly reduce the need for other methods of weed control. In the small-scale Indonesian study referenced previously,[85] black plastic mulch reduced the time required for weeding stevia plots by more than 73%. Manual weed control and a

---

[82] Data from http://www.weather.com/weather/wxclimatology/monthly/graph/LOXX0004. (accessed July 2, 2010).

[83] В.М. Завгородній [Zavgorodniy]; Источник: Автореф. дис... канд. с.-г. наук: 06.01.09 /; Ін-т цукр. буряків УААН.—К., 2006.—20 с.—укр. ОПТИМІЗАЦІЯ ЕЛЕМЕНТІВ ТЕХНОЛОГІЇ ВИРОЩУВАННЯ СТЕВІЇ В УМОВАХ ЛІСОСТЕПУ УКРАЇНИ. ІНСТИТУТ ЦУКРОВИХ БУРЯКІВ УКРАЇНСЬКОЇ АКАДЕМІЇ АГРАРНИХ НАУК. ["Optimization of Technology of Cultivation of Stevia Under Conditions of Steppes of Ukraine"] http://disser.com.ua/contents/15348.html.

[84] A. Hegazi, "Plastic Mulching for Weed Control and Water Economy in Vineyards," *ISHS Acta Horticulturae 536: 14th International Synposium on Horticultural Economics,* 2000.

[85] Basuki and Sumaryono, "Effect of black plastic mulch and plant density"

planting density of 500 plants/24 m² (20.8/m², 208,000/ha, or 84,211/acre) were used. Results were as follows:

Using black plastic mulch, weeding required:
About 136 minutes/24 m²/year (944 hr./ha or 382 hr./acre)

Without using any mulch, weeding required:
About 521 minutes/24 m²/year (3618 hr./ha or 1465 hr./acre)

Extrapolating from this study, mulching with black plastic would save about 2674 hours of weeding/ha/year (1083 hours/acre), assuming manual weeding. The potential savings in labor cost for weeding should be considered when deciding on the use of plastic mulch, in addition to the potential for higher yields as shown in figures 24 and 25.

Organic mulch can also provide a weed control benefit. Trials described in the Journal of Sustainable Agriculture compared various mulching options for non-mechanized small-scale tomato production.[86] Hay mulch was applied at 100 mm (4 in.) depth several weeks after transplanting to the field. Annual weed control was good and sometimes resulted in a net labor savings compared to unmulched plots. Seeds carried in the hay mulch contributed to perennial weeds in only one of eight plots. Two layers of newspaper placed under hay or straw mulch enhanced weed control effectiveness. Since the planting density for stevia is higher than for tomatoes, more labor would likely be required for manual weeding. This might give mulching a bigger advantage.

---

[86] Mark W. Schonbeck, "Weed Suppression and Labor Costs Associated with Organic, Plastic, and paper Mulches in Small-Scale Vegetable Production," *Journal of Sustainable Agriculture* 13, no. 2 (1999): 13–33.

The soil-warming effect of black plastic mulch might be expected to provide a benefit in climates with short growing seasons or cool springs. But in the Indonesian study, black plastic mulch boosted yield even in a tropical climate with consistently warm temperatures (18°C–26°C or 64.4°F–78.8°F).[87] Organic mulch such as hay or straw might provide a soil cooling benefit where summers are extremely hot, even though stevia generally likes warmth.

The cost of using mulch films will vary widely depending on material costs, machinery efficiency, and labor costs. In a 2002 publication, the University of California estimated a cost of US $450 per acre ($1112 per ha) including labor.[88] This is for 4 ft. (122 cm) wide plastic on 60 in. (152 cm) wide beds using 1.5 mil plastic. A 2004 fact sheet from the Oklahoma Cooperative Extension Service estimated a cost of US $275–$300 per acre ($679–$741 per ha) including installation and removal of plastic mulch.[89] Check with mulch vendors, extension agents, or university horticulture specialist for current costs.

Weed Control

Good weed control is critical for a stevia crop. Because of the lack of registered herbicides for stevia,[90] mechanical or manual weed control will likely be necessary. Even if herbi-

---

[87] Basuki and Sumaryono, "Effect of black plastic mulch and plant density"
[88] Wayne L. Schrader, Jose L. Aguiar, and Keith S. Mayberry, "Cucumber Production in California," Publication 8050, University of California Agriculture and Natural Resources, 2002. http://ucanr.org/freepubs/docs/8050.pdf.
[89] Dean McCraw and James E. Motes. 2004. "Use of Plastic Mulch and Row Covers in Vegetable Production, HLA-6034." Oklahoma Cooperative Extension Service.
http://pods.dasnr.okstate.edu/docushare/dsweb/Services/Document-1099
[90] See Columbus, "Stevia," in *Richters Second Conference*, 3–10.

cides are made available for stevia, using them might disqualify a crop for organic certification.

Mike Columbus recommends commencing weeding early in the season and repeating every 7–10 days. Farmers in Canada used tractor-mounted cultivation equipment adapted to the row spacing of the crop.[91] With stevia's shallow root system, older plants might be damaged by tractor cultivation close to the plants. Some manual hand hoeing or pulling will likely be necessary.

An Indonesian study showed manual weed control would require about 3618 hours of labor/ha/year (1465 hr./acre) on stevia fields with a high planting density and without mulch. The same study showed an approximate 73% reduction in manual weeding time when black plastic sheets were used as a mulch.[92] Mulching with plastic or paper sheets can be a big help for weed control. Organic mulches such as straw or hay can also help. See the "mulching" section above for more about using mulch for weed control.

Farmers in Canada found weeding to be one of their largest costs of production. In fields without mulch, one farmer paid over Can $1200 for weed control on a per-hectare basis, including a combination of tractor cultivation and manual hoeing.[93]

Row Covers

Row covers create a warm microclimate around plants, getting them off to a faster start where spring nights are cold.

---

[91] Ibid.
[92] Basuki and Sumaryono, "Effect of black plastic mulch and plant density"
[93] See Columbus, "Stevia," in *Richters Second Conference*, 3–10.

Row covers are usually designed to be used on growing beds, covering the width of the bed. "Low tunnels" often consist of slitted plastic sheets over wire hoops. "High Tunnels" are much larger versions with a permanent frame. They cover the width of multiple growing beds or rows. High tunnels are initially more expensive than low tunnels, but might be ideal for plant propagation or overwintering mother plants in some climates. Typically, people and tractors can work inside a high tunnel.

Small-scale stevia trials using an annual production cycle near Bonn, Germany (lat 50.6°N) showed a significant yield increase from using plastic high tunnels. This makes sense because stevia plants typically get off to a slow start with cold night temperatures and cold soils. Black plastic mulch and/or plastic tunnels can raise soil and air temperatures near plants.

Various types of row cover material are available. A slitted plastic film is most often used. The slits provide ventilation. Various newer permeable row cover materials will allow air and rainfall through the material, while still providing a warmer microclimate around plants. For low tunnels, the cover material is usually supported by heavy wire or conduit in a hoop shape. For large-scale plantings, machines are available to install wire hoops and row cover.

Temperatures inside tunnels should be monitored carefully. When temperatures routinely exceed about 90°F (32°C) inside the tunnels, I would recommend additional venting or removal of covers.

Costs and benefits

Figure 26 shows dried stevia leaf yield using high tunnels and without high tunnels at three different planting densities in small-scale trials near Bonn, Germany. Figure 27 lists the yield and gross income increases resulting from the use of plastic high tunnels in these same trials. The lowest yield increase was 723 lb. dried leaf/acre/year at a planting density of 44,519 plants/acre.[94] Assuming you get US $2 per pound, this would translate to about US $1446 additional gross income per acre due to using plastic high tunnels. Keep in mind this is a single study with particular climatic and other conditions. Results might be different on your farm and at a larger scale. Trials can be used to determine whether plastic tunnels are profitable on your farm.

Labor and material costs for plastic high tunnels will vary considerably over time and by location. For large areas, Haygrove brand high tunnels might cost US $26,000–$28,000 per acre for initial installation.[95] These are permanent structures, but the plastic covering must be replaced periodically.

Low tunnels, designed to cover the width of one growing bed, might be an option as well. The plastic can be removed when the warmest part of the summer arrives. A 2002 publication from the University of California estimates a cost for low tunnels of US $1000 per acre including labor.[96] This is for a standard low tunnel with 1.5 mil plastic on 60 in. (152 cm) wide beds.

---

[94] Pude, Schmitz-Eiberger, and Noga, "Development, Yield"
[95] George DeVault. "Farming under cover – BIG TIME!" Rodale Institute. http://newfarm.rodaleinstitute.org/columns/george_devault/2004/0804/haygrove.shtml (accessed July 2, 2010).
[96] Schrader, Aguiar, and Mayberry, *Cucumber Production in California*

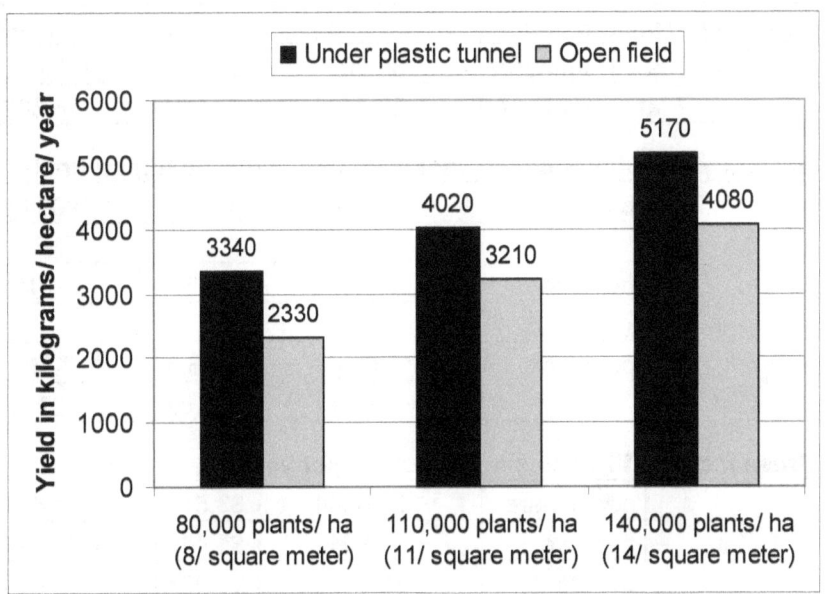

Figure 26: Dry leaf yield under plastic high tunnels versus open field.[97] *Yield in one year from small-scale trials with annual production cycle near Bonn, Germany (lat 50.6°N).*

---

[97] Data from Pude, Schmitz-Eiberger, and Noga, "Development, Yield"

Plants per square meter:	8	11	14
Plants per hectare:	80,000	110,000	140,000
Plants per acre:	32,377	44,519	56,660
Dry leaf yield difference per year from use of plastic high tunnels			
per hectare:	+ 1010 kg	+ 810 kg	+ 1090 kg
per acre:	+ 902 lbs	+ 723 lbs	+ 972 lbs
per plant:	+ 12.63 g	+ 7.36 g	+ 7.79 g
	+ .45 oz	+ .26 oz	+ .27 oz
Gross income difference in US dollars per year at $2 per pound			
per hectare:	+ $4,454	+ $3,572	+ $4,807
per acre:	+ $1,804	+ $1,446	+ $1,944
per plant:	+ $0.056	+ $0.033	+ $0.034

Figure 27: Yield and gross income differences from using plastic high tunnels.[98] *As compared to open field, from small-scale stevia trials with an annual production cycle near Bonn, Germany (lat 50.6°N).*

Plant Pruning

Left alone, most stevia genotypes produce tall stems with little branching. Pruning can encourage greater branching, better leaf production, and less lodging of stems due to wind. Tip pruning forces branching by removing the growing tip from a stem. The usual procedure is to pinch or cut 2–3 in. from stem tips. Pruning is especially important if plants produce blossom buds early on, but the benefits can be realized even when blossoming has not begun.

---

[98] Data from Pude, Schmitz-Eiberger, and Noga, "Development, Yield"

Costs and benefits

A study near Kiev, Ukraine (lat about 50°N) found pinching (tip pruning) to be profitable under the conditions of the study.[99] An increase in dry leaf yield of 2150 kg/ha (1920 lb/acre) was obtained by pinching stem tips once at 35 days from transplanting to the field. This was at the beginning of intensive plant growth. The study achieved a total dry leaf yield of 5430 kg/ha (4849 lb/acre) with pinching, black plastic film mulch and a planting density of 80,000 plants/ha.

Tip pruning is done by hand. Cost will depend on the cost of labor and the skill level of workers. Based on labor costs in your region, a determination can be made whether pruning might provide an economic benefit. For plants in annual production or the first year of a perennial production cycle, I recommend tip pruning three times during the first half of the growing season. This assumes sufficient labor is available. The Ukrainian study showed even a single pruning provided a significant boost in yield.

It makes sense that the greatest benefit from pruning would be realized with lower planting densities. With higher planting densities (closer plant spacing), plants might tend to support one another against the wind. Also, fewer stems on each plant would be required to occupy the smaller available growing space.

In the case of a perennial production cycle, a lower planting density might be used in order to allow room for plant

---

[99] See В.М. Завгородній [Zavgorodniy]; Источник: Автореф. дис... канд. с.-г. наук: 06.01.09 /; Ін-т цукр. буряків УААН.—К., 2006.—20 с.— укр. ОПТИМІЗАЦІЯ ЕЛЕМЕНТІВ ТЕХНОЛОГІЇ ВИРОЩУВАННЯ СТЕВІЇ В УМОВАХ ЛІСОСТЕПУ УКРАЇНИ. ІНСТИТУТ ЦУКРОВИХ БУРЯКІВ УКРАЇНСЬКОЇ АКАДЕМІЇ АГРАРНИХ НАУК. ["Optimization of Technology of Cultivation of Stevia Under Conditions of Steppes of Ukraine"]

expansion in later years. In this case, tip pruning in the first year would probably be beneficial, but might not be needed as much in subsequent years. Older plants tend to naturally send up multiple stems from the crown, better filling the available growing space without pruning. An exception could be made in locations close to the equator where short days encourage quick blossoming. Tip pruning should help delay blossoming, thereby increasing leaf production.

Figure 28: Plants branching after pruning.

Nutrient Deficiencies and Toxicities

Researchers in Brazil studied symptoms of nutrient deficiencies and toxicities in *Stevia rebaudiana*. In summary form, findings included the following symptoms:[100]

- **Nitrogen deficiency:** Reduced development. Smaller leaves. Fewer branches. General yellowing.

- **Phosphorus deficiency:** Reduced growth.

- **Potassium deficiency:** Drooping leaves that seem to have lower water content. Initially darker leaves. Fewer branches. After 3–4 weeks, yellowing and necrosis of older leaves, starting at the leaf apex.

- **Calcium deficiency:** Starts with dark spots at leaf apex of young leaves. Spots expand. Chlorosis with dark brown spots on older leaves. Wilting and collapse of upper stem.

- **Magnesium deficiency:** Older leaves from the second harvest sometimes exhibited paling due to very low magnesium levels. Chlorosis began at leaf base, forming a "V" shape.

- **Sulfur deficiency:** No symptoms were observed, but there was a significant reduction in the production of leaves and shoots.

- **Boron deficiency:** Symptoms appear with severe deficiency. Reduced root growth with thickening, branching, and darkening. Thickening younger leaves. Chlorosis in and around leaf ribs, with reddish tint. Deformed leaves. Cracking stems.

---

[100] Lima Filho, O. F. de and MALAVOLTA, E., "SINTOMAS DE DESORDENS NUTRICIONAIS EM ESTÉVIA Stevia rebaudiana (Bert.) Bertoni." ["Symptoms of Nutritional Disorders in Stevia (Stevia rebaudiana)"] *Scientia Agricola* 54, 1-2 (1997): 53-61.

- **Boron toxicity:** Spots on edges and tips of older leaves followed by brown and black banding and chlorosis plus browning of leaf tip and then the entire leaf. Symptoms spread to younger leaves.
- **Zinc toxicity:** Necrotic leaf spots of irregular size and shape, usually starting in the center of the older leaves, progressing to younger leaves. Eventual necrosis of the whole leaf followed by plant wilting and death. No symptoms were observed with zinc deficiency.

Another source indicates boron deficiency sometimes causes leaf spot in stevia. They recommend spraying Borax at 6% as a remedy.[101]

Laboratory analysis can help in identifuing deficiencies, toxicities, and diseases. Agricultural university and extension agents can help arrange plant tissue and soil analyses.

Pests and Diseases

Pests and diseases are not major problems for stevia in most locations. As production grows around the world, however, this could change. Crop rotation is a good precaution for preventing disease problems in field production. Crop rotation means that a crop, or group of closely related crops, is moved from one field to another on a 3–5 year cycle. This way, pests and diseases do not have a chance to build up in fields. Stevia is in the Asteraceae/Compositae family,[102] same as sunflowers, marigolds, lettuce, zinnia, daisies, and asters. In

---

[101] Farooqi and Sreeramu, *Cultivation of medicinal*, 636.
[102] For more information on the taxonomy of stevia, see the USDA ARS Germplasm Resources Information Network at http://www.ars-grin.gov/cgi-bin/npgs/html/taxon.pl?35581#syn.

general, plants in the same family are susceptible to the same pests and diseases.

If a disease appears, there may be a biological or low-toxicity measure available for control. The appendix lists dealers of pest and disease control products. A good place to start, especially for identification, is your local university extension service or agricultural university.

Egyptian researchers studied commercial chemical fungicides for use on *Stevia rebaudiana*:

> Two commercial fungicides, Topsin M [thiophanate-methyl] 70% WP and Vitavax [carboxin]/Thiram 75% WP (at 3 g/litre water or 3 g/kg seeds), and 2 biocides, Plant Guard (Trichoderma harzianum at 3 × 107 cfu/ml) and Rhizo N (Bacillus subtilis at 3 × 107 cfu/ml) applied as dip treatment or seed dressing, were evaluated for their effectiveness in controlling soil borne fungal pathogens. Topsin M was the most effective in controlling the majority of soil borne fungi, while Plant Guard had greater efficacy than the other fungicides only in controlling F. oxysporum. Plant Guard was not effective against R. solani and Sclerotium rolfsii, and Rhizo N was not effective against R. solani.[103]

Some diseases, such as septoria, are passed along through vegetative propagation. Septoria leaf spot has been a significant problem in Canadian field production. Unfortunately, the fungicide sprays that work against septoria tend to leave high levels of residue and would not qualify for organic production.[104] The best solution for septoria may be propagation from

---

[103] Arafa A. Hilal and Mohamed A. Baiuomy, "First record of fungal diseases of stevia (Stevia rebaudiana Bertoni) in Egypt," *Egypt. J. Agric. Res.* 78, no. 4 (2000): 1435–1448.

[104] Brandle, "Stevia," in *Richters Third Commercial Herb Growing*

seed or the selection of resistant strains for vegetative propagation. I do not know of resistant varieties available to the public, but farmers can try selecting plants that seem unaffected and propagate those by stem cuttings.

Researcher Clinton Shock at Davis, California reported serious slug damage on stevia shoots emerging from winter dormancy in the spring.[105] Davis is located near Sacramento, in USDA plant hardiness zone 9b. In this climate, stevia tops die back from frost over the winter, but sprout back from the roots in the spring.

I have heard of serious deer damage on stevia, but I have also heard of instances where deer seem to avoid stevia plants. Rabbits are another potential pest. However, I have not noticed significant damage to my own plants despite a population of wild rabbits in the vicinity.

Greenhouse production

Pests and disease can become troublesome in the confined spaces and warm, humid conditions of a greenhouse. This can affect stevia plug production or overwintering stevia plants. Aphids, thrips, scale, mites, and whiteflies may be controlled with insecticidal soap, horticultural oil, or beneficial insects such as ladybugs and lacewings.

A greenhouse grower of stevia transplants in Missouri (US) reported a greenhouse infestation of broad mites (*Polyphagotarsonemus latus*) on young stevia plants grown from stem cuttings. Broad mites are too small to be visible with the naked eye. Brown growing tips are typical of mite damage. The broad mites were successfully controlled by spraying with

---

[105] Shock, "Experimental Cultivation of Rebaudi's Stevia"

insecticidal soap—a mixture of water, rubbing alcohol, and dish soap.[106]

Soil-born fungal diseases can be prevented or minimized by using a growing medium with a biofungicide. Steve Marsden switched to PRO-MIX 'BX'/MYCORISE® PRO as a medium for rooting stevia stem cuttings after experiencing problems with pythium disease.[107] "We have switched our growing medium," said Marsden, "to Premier BX with MYCORISE® PRO. This is a natural soil fungus that helps the roots of plants grow better."[108]

Diseases reported on stevia

A search of horticultural journals can reveal the latest information about diseases reported on stevia throughout the world. These diseases include Powdery mildew, Damping-off, Stem rot *(Sclerotium)*, Leaf Spot *(Alternaria)*, Gray mold *(Botrytis)*, Root rot *(Sclerotium)*, Septoria leaf spot, *Verticillium dahliae*, and Tomato Spotted Wilt Virus (TSWV). Following is a listing of diseases reported on stevia and some report summaries:

- Powdery mildew *(Erysiphe cichoracearum DC)*[109]
- Damping-off *(Rhizoctonia solani Kuehn)*[110]

---

[106] From author's correspondence with grower Steve Marsden of Herbal Advantage Inc. (www.herbaladvantage.com). Broad mites were detected by the Extension Plant Diagnostic Clinic at the University of Missouri; 23 Mumford Hall; Columbia, MO 65211. PlantSci@missouri.edu. Also see comments at: http://www.theherbalinsider.com/archives/80.

[107] For information and to locate distributors, see: http://www.premierhort.com/eProMix/Horticulture/Products/GrowingMediaCat/Biofungicide/fSubtilex.htm.

[108] See comments at: http://www.theherbalinsider.com/archives/80.

[109] Reported in Thomas S. C. Li, *Medicinal Plants–Culture, Utilization and Phytopharmacology* (Lancaster, PA: Technomic Publishing, 2000).

[110] Ibid.

- Leaf spot (*Alternaria*) in the region of South Bengal, India during February with temperatures of 20°C –25°C.
    ...severe foliar infections were observed... Symptoms initially appeared as small circular spots, light brown in colour. Later, many became irregular and dark brown to grey, while others remained circular with concentric rings or zones... Leaf spots varied from 2–18 mm in diameter.[111]

- Gray mold caused by *Botrytis cinerea* in Italy on 3 month old plants, watered by sprinkle irrigation, in a greenhouse on heated benches with temperatures of 16–20°C.
    Leaves, starting from the basal ones, showed small, brown spots that spread across the entire leaf surface. Subsequently, the crown and stem were infected, and the pathogen developed abundant, soft, gray mycelium on leaves and stems...[112]

- Root rot caused by *Sclerotium rolfsii* in stevia-producing villages of Erode district in Tamil Nadu State of India, between June and September 2005 on 2 month old stevia plants.
    Symptoms first appeared as yellowing and drooping of leaves, with wilting of plants and white cottony mycelial growth at the collar region. The mycelial growth spread to the stem and roots, with associated tissue rotting. On the diseased areas, brown sclerotia were observed.[113]

- Septoria leaf spot (*Septoria steviae*) in British Columbia and Ontario, Canada in 1995.
    Symptoms included depressed, angular, shiny olive-gray foliar lesions that rapidly coalesced and were often sur-

---

[111] C. K. Maiti, S. Sen, R. Acharya, and K. Acharya, "First report of Alternaria alternata causing leaf spot on Stevia rebaudiana," *Plant Pathology* 56, no. 4 (2007): 723.

[112] A Garibaldi, D Bertetti, P Pensa, and M L Gullino, "First Report of Gray Mold Caused by Botrytis cinerea on Stevia rebaudiana in Italy," *Plant Disease : an International Journal of Applied Plant Pathology* 93, no. 3 (2009): 318.

[113] A. Kamalakannan, V. Valluvaparidasan, K. Chitra, E. Rajeswari, K. Salaheddin, D. Ladhalakshmi, and A. Chandrasekaran, "First report of root rot of stevia caused by Sclerotium rolfsii in India," *Plant Pathology* 56, no. 2 (2007): 350.

rounded by a chlorotic halo. Leaves quickly became necrotic and often dropped off the plant.[114]

- Stem rot (*Sclerotium dephinii* Welch)[115]
- Stem rot (*Sclerotinia sclerotiorum*) at the Crop Diversification Centre South; Brooks, Alberta; in August, 1996 on 4 month old plants when plants reached about 30 cm.
  Diseased stems showed dark brown lesions above and at soil level… Under dry conditions, mild stem lesions caused plant stunting with lower leaves turning black and curling downward… The entire plant collapsed when girdling of the crown and roots occurred. Superficial white mycelium developed over the basal part of affected stems under moist conditions, especially after rainy periods.[116]
- *Verticillium dahliae* in California, US, October 1999.
  …stevia plants in a commercial field exhibited stunting, leaf necrosis, and vascular discoloration.[117]
- Tomato Spotted Wilt Virus (TSWV) in northern Greece in June, 2006.
  …virus-like symptoms similar to those caused by TSWV were observed on sweet honey leaf (Stevia rebaudiana (Bertoni) Bertoni, [synonym Eupatorium rebaudianum Bertoni], family Asteraceae) plants and on potato (Solanum tuberosum, family Solanaceae) plants growing close to tobacco. Diseased S. rebaudiana plants expressed chlorotic and necrotic rings and line patterns on systemically infected leaves and occasionally a general chlorosis or dwarfing of the plant. Potato plants ex-

---

[114] N. M. Lovering and R. D. Reeleder, "First report of Septoria steviae on Stevia (Stevia rebaudiana) in North America," *Plant Disease* 80, no. 8 (1996): 959.

[115] Ibid.

[116] K. F. Chang, R. J. Howard, et al., "First report of stevia as a host of Sclerotinia sclerotiorum," *Plant Disease* 81, no. 3 (1997): 311.

[117] J. J. Farrar, R. M. Davis, et al., "First report of Verticillium dahliae on stevia (Stevia rebaudiana) in North America," *Plant Disease* August 84, no. 8 (2000): 922. Department of Plant Pathology, University of California, Davis.

pressed only necrotic rings or lesions and a mild plant dwarfing. Seven percent of the S. rebaudiana plants, but only 0.1% of the potato plants, were showing symptoms.[118]

- "Soilborne diseases such as southern blight caused by *Sclerotium rolfsii* [*Corticium rolfsii*]; charcoal rot caused by *Macrophomina phaseolina*; wilt caused by *Fusarium oxysporum*; root rot caused by *F. semitectum* [*F. pallidoroseum*], *F. solani* and *Rhizoctonia solani*; as well as airborne diseases such as black spot caused by *Alternaria steviae* and grey mould caused by *Botrytis cinerea* were recorded for the first time on Stevia rebaudiana plants growing in Egypt... Sclerotium rolfsii is the most virulent pathogen, followed by F. oxysporum, M. phaseolina and R. solani."[119]

---

[118] E. K. Chatzivassilou, D. Peters, and P. Lolas, "Occurrence of Tomato spotted wilt virus in Stevia rebaudiana and Solanum tuberosum in Northern Greece," *Plant Disease -St Paul* 91 no. 9 (2007): 1205.

[119] Hilal and Baiuomy, "First record of fungal diseases of stevia in Egypt"

Chapter 4

Field Planting

Planting Density

Most growers probably use a planting density of eighty thousand (80,000) plants/ha or less (about 32,000 plants/acre). As with other factors, on-farm trials can be used to determine the most profitable planting density (number of plant in a given area) for your location. Trials by university researchers seem to indicate profits could be improved with higher planting densities.

Costs and benefits of high planting densities

With small-scale trials, researchers at Bonn University in Germany (lat 50.6°N) tested three different planting densities in the open field and under plastic high tunnels. This was an annual production cycle in a climate with cold winters, warm summers, and long summer days.[120] In the case of open field production, a planting density of 14 plants/m^2 (140,000/ha) resulted in the highest dry leaf yield per hectare (see fig. 26).

---

[120] Pude, Schmitz-Eiberger, and Noga, "Development, Yield"

This highest planting density also resulted in a dry leaf yield per plant that is virtually the same as from lower planting densities (see fig. 29, gray bars). For open field production under the conditions present, these trials indicate a clear profitability advantage for the highest planting density, no matter what the cost of transplants might be.

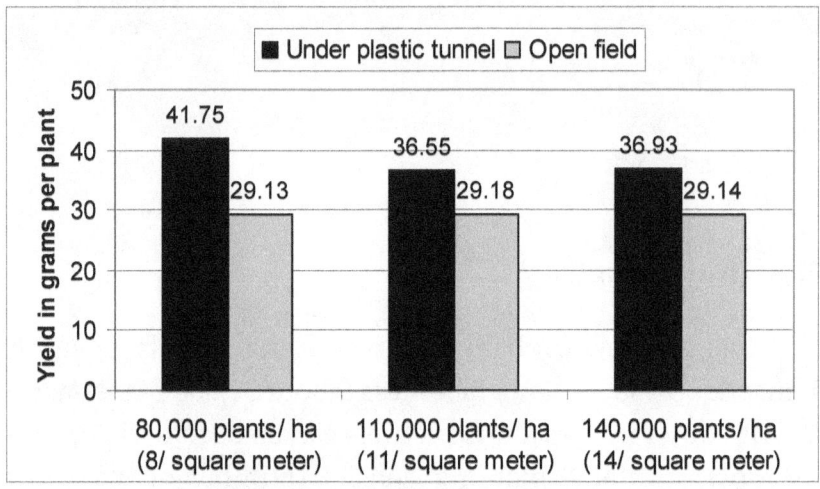

Figure 29: Dry leaf yield per plant by planting density.[121]
Yield in one year extrapolated from small-scale field trials with an annual production cycle near Bonn, Germany (lat 50.6°N).

The German trials showed significantly higher yields under plastic high tunnels as compared to open field production (see fig. 26 and 29, compare black and gray bars). Using plastic high tunnels, the highest planting density (14 plants/m²) produced the highest yield per hectare (see fig. 26, black bars). However, the lowest planting density (8 plants/m²) produced the highest yield per plant (see fig. 29, black bars). This means the lowest planting density achieved the lowest transplant cost

---

[121] Ibid.

for a given unit of leaf harvest. But the highest planting density (14 plants/m^2) is probably the most profitable choice under all conditions tested—even under plastic high tunnels. Why? Even with an unlimited supply of land, costs such as labor, irrigation, tractor fuel, and high tunnels will be higher per unit of yield with a lower planting density. These higher costs would likely outweigh lower plant costs. In most cases, maximizing yield per unit of land is the most profitable approach.

Using yield data from the German trials and assuming US $2 income per pound of dry leaf, figure 30 shows the annual yield and income differences resulting from a planting density of 14 plants/m^2 as compared to 8 plants/m^2.

Dry leaf yield difference per year with 14 plants per square meter as compared to 8 plants per square meter			
		open field	with high tunnels
	per hectare:	+ 1750 kg	+ 1830 kg
	per acre:	+ 1561 lb.	+ 1634 lb.
	per plant:	No difference	– 4.84 g
			– .18 oz.
Gross income difference in US dollars per year at $2 per pound			
	per hectare:	+ $7,718	+ $8,070
	per acre:	+ $3,122	+ $3,268
	per plant:	No difference	– $0.023

Figure 30: Dry leaf yield and gross income differences from using a high planting density.[122] *At 14 plants/m² as compared to 8 plants/m², extrapolated from small-scale trials with an annual production cycle near Bonn, Germany (lat 50.6°N).*

Keep in mind these German trials were for an annual production cycle in a temperate climate. Results may be different for perennial production. As plant roots grow larger in the second and subsequent years of a perennial production cycle, lower planting densities may capture the yield advantage. Also, higher planting densities may bring about crowding and disease pressure in the later years of a perennial production cycle.

A study conducted in Indonesia also observed the highest dried leaf yield/hectare/year from the highest planting density.[123] This is a tropical climate capable of perennial produc-

---

[122] Ibid.
[123] Basuki and Sumaryono, "Effect of black plastic mulch and plant density"

tion and a much longer growing season as compared to Germany. However, this study considered only the first year of a perennial production cycle. Results are illustrated in figure 32. Yields were much higher at about 133,000 plants/ha as compared to 40,000 plants/ha. At about 208,000 plants/ha without mulch, yields were only slightly higher than at 133,000 plants/ha. Considering the cost of plants and the practical difficulties of extremely close planting, it seems about 133,000 plants/ha would be the optimum planting density under the conditions of this Indonesian study.

Figure 31 gives an idea of the plant spacing necessary for the three planting densities used in the German trials. It also gives yields and unit conversions for each planting density. Some tractor-drawn transplanters might not be capable of the close plant spacing necessary for high planting densities.

Plants per square meter:	8	11	14
Plants per hectare:	80,000	110,000	140,000
Plants per acre:	32,377	44,519	56,660
Grid pattern spacing:	35x35 cm	30x30 cm	27x27 cm
	14x14 in.	12x12 in.	11x11 in.
Standard row spacing options:	46x27 cm	41x22 cm	36x20 cm
	18x11 in.	16x9 in.	14x8 in.

Spacing options in beds, 4 rows per bed

Between bed centers:	64 in.	64 in.	64 in.
	163 cm	163 cm	163 cm
Between rows in bed:	12 in.	12 in.	12 in.
	30 cm	30 cm	30 cm
In-row spacing:	12 in.	8.5 in.	7 in.
	30 cm	22 cm	17 cm

Dry leaf yield in German trials with annual production cycle

Open field per hectare:	2330 kg	3210 kg	4080 kg
With plastic high tunnels per hectare:	3340 kg	4020 kg	5170 kg
Open field per acre:	943 kg	1299 kg	1651 kg
	2079 lb.	2864 lb.	3640 lb.
With plastic high tunnels per acre:	1350 kg	1630 kg	2090 kg
	2976 lb.	3594 lb.	4608 lb.
Open field per plant:	29 g	29 g	29 g
	1.03 oz.	1.03 oz.	1.03 oz.
With plastic high tunnels per plant:	42 g	37 g	37 g
	1.47 oz.	1.29 oz.	1.30 oz.

Figure 31: Plant spacing options, unit conversions, & yields.
Yield data from small-scale trials near Bonn, Germany.[124]

---

[124] Data derived from Pude, Schmitz-Eiberger, and Noga, "Development, Yield"

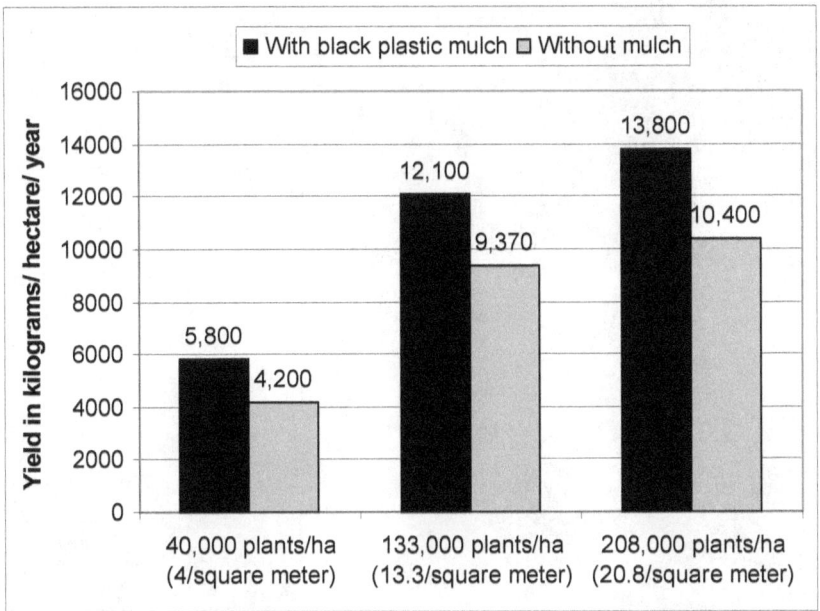

Figure 32: Approximate dry leaf yield at various planting densities in a tropical climate.[125] *Based on extrapolation from first-year harvest from small-scale field trials with a perennial production cycle near Sukabumi, West Java, Indonesia (about lat 7°S).*

---

[125] Basuki and Sumaryono, "Effect of black plastic mulch and plant density"

Figure 33: Young stevia plants grown on raised beds.
Photo provided by Sunfruits Ltd. in India. Used with permission.
http://www.sunfruit.biz/.

Transplanting to the Field

If you will not be starting your own transplants, you may want to seek out a local greenhouse for custom growing. Also, several mail order nurseries have perfected packaging that allows successful shipment of plants. Check the appendix for stevia plant suppliers. For a large number of plants, you will usually need to place an order well in advance.

Most farmers use plants grown as "plugs." This means each plant is grown in its own small pot or "cell." A "flat" of plugs usually includes 72–120 plugs. Plugs survive well, with minimal transplant shock, and work well with tractor-drawn transplanters.

Try to transplant on a cloudy day or in the evening. Set plants a little deeper than they were in the pot. Avoid walking or kneeling on growing beds. Irrigate with a gentle soaking soon after transplanting. Plants tend to grow slowly at first and accelerate as weather warms.

For larger fields, tractor-drawn transplanting implements are available. Some models form a hole and put a dose of water in the hole. Some are designed to poke a hole through mulching films. A plant is placed in each hole by machine or hand. Vendors of transplanting implements are listed in the appendix. You may be able to rent a machine or find used transplanters in your area.

Researcher Mike Columbus reported that a Canadian farmer was able to finish transplanting to a 2½-acre field (about 1 ha) in eight hours with a three-row tractor-drawn transplanter and four workers.[126] Three people were on the transplanter and one driving the tractor. The planting density was 40,000 plants/acre (a total of 100,000 plants for 2½ acres).

---

[126] Columbus, "Stevia," in *Richters Second Conference*, 5.

Chapter 5

Harvesting and Postharvest

Dried leaf is the basic stevia commodity produced by farmers. It may be shipped to the end wholesale or retail buyer. With the proper equipment, dried stevia leaves may be further processed for value added products such as tea cut or powdered stevia leaf.

Techniques for harvesting, drying, and leaf separation will vary depending on the size of the field and the amount of mechanization used. For small plots, most of the work will be done by hand. Even for larger fields, the work may be done by hand if affordable labor is available. Manual labor is likely to produce the highest-quality end product. But machines can substitute for labor to some extent. Stevia is a fairly new crop for large-scale production. Farmers will need to adapt or build machinery to harvest and dry stevia leaves. I will describe techniques for small plots and hand labor, but also introduce ideas for mechanization and larger-scale production.

Tools and techniques vary, but the basic steps for turning a field of stevia into saleable dried stevia leaves are as follows:

Steps for Harvesting Stevia

1. **Cutting and Gathering.** Cut stems with leaves and transport to the drying area.

2. **Drying.** Dry leaves and stems together soon after cutting.

3. **Leaf Separation.** Separate leaves from stems.

4. **Storage and Shipping.** Pack leaves for storage or shipping.

Figure 34: Stevia blossoms and blossom buds.

Cutting and Gathering

See chapter 1 for complete information about harvest timing for dried leaves based on blossom timing at various latitudes. Generally, the highest leaf yield is obtained by harvesting when blossom buds first begin to form or shortly before the usual blossoming date. Trials in the Czech Republic (about lat 50°N) indicated the highest overall yield of stevioside (a sweet glycoside) could be obtained by cutting in early September, a few weeks before blossoming.[127]

Blossom bud timing depends mainly on the day length at your latitude. In very low latitudes (closest to the equator),

---

[127] Nepovim et al., "The effect of cultivation conditions"

blossoming may be nearly continuous, requiring more frequent harvests, possibly during the early stages of blossoming. A disease outbreak may be another reason for earlier harvesting or multiple harvests per growing season.

In very high latitudes or high altitudes, cold temperatures might force harvesting before plant blossoming begins. Mature plant tops can survive temperatures a few degrees under freezing, however. Canadian researcher Mike Columbus found that mature plants might survive temperatures as low as 21.2°F (−6°C) in the fall.[128]

Field cutting should be done when plants are dry—free of dew or any moisture. Cut entire stevia stems at 4–6 in. (10–15 cm) above ground level. If plants will be allowed to re-grow, trials in California showed a six-inch (15.2 cm) cutting height resulted in better plant survival and better yield in later cuttings as compared to a two-inch (5 cm) cutting height.[129]

For annual production with only one cutting, a lower cutting height should produce a greater leaf yield.[130] However, sometimes the lowest leaves are excessively dirty or affected by disease. In this case, a higher cutting height can help exclude poorer-quality leaves.

Try to exclude dirt or foreign material from the harvested material as much as possible. Mechanized harvesting methods should be designed so the quality of harvested leaves is optimized and contamination is minimized. Ideally, harvested material should get from the field to the drying area without touching the ground. Following are ideas for cutting and gathering tools:

---

[128] Columbus, "Stevia," in *Richters Second Conference*, 5.
[129] Shock, "Experimental Cultivation of Rebaudi's Stevia"
[130] Ibid.

- Hedge shears or sheep shears (hand tools)
- Sickle or reaping hook (hand tools)
- Catching scythe (hand tool)
- Herb harvester with engine-power cutter bar on wheels (pushed by hand)
- Modified peanut harvester, grain reaper, or other modified machines (tractor-towed)
- Herb harvester-mower machines (self-propelled or tractor towed with integrated cutting and collecting)

Hand-harvested stems can be placed on a cart, tarp, or sheet for transport to the drying area or to a wagon or truck for longer-distance transport. A large amount of harvested material can be moved by hand in a sheet. Tie the corners of the sheet around the pile of stems to make a bundle.

In *Herbal Harvest,* author Greg Whitten Recommends a "catching scythe" for cutting and gathering herbs.[131] A manual grain-cutting scythe is fitted with a "catcher" made from metal mesh "chicken wire" on a wire frame. The catcher holds cut material which can then be deposited on a nearby sheet. This is probably the quickest hand-powered method of harvesting without letting cut material touch the ground.

---

[131] Greg Whitten, *Herbal Harvest: Commercial Organic Production of Quality Dried Herbs, third edition.* (Melbourne, Australia: Blooming Books, 2004) 121–125.

Figure 35: HT-Cala Harvester from Jenquip. *Photo provided by Jenquip and used with permission. www.jenquip.co.nz.*

A possibility for reasonably priced mechanization might be an engine-powered cutter bar mounted on wheels as in figure 35. This is the *HT-Cala Harvester* from Jenquip in New Zealand.[132] There is no record that Jenquip harvesters have been used for harvesting stevia. But Merv George of Jenquip believes this machine, designed for tall calla stems, would work for cutting stevia.[133] The cutter height is adjustable and controls are conveniently located. George suggests a collection tray might be added directly behind the cutter bar. When the collection tray is full, the rig would be stopped and the material transferred to a trailer for transport to the drying area.

---

[132] Jenquip web site: www.jenquip.co.nz.
[133] Merv George, personal correspondence, 2009.

Figure 36: Jenquip herb harvester with infeed reel.
HT-KumaP c/w infeed reel. Photo provided by Jenquip and used with permission. www.jenquip.co.nz.

Because the *HT-Cala harvester* lacks an infeed reel to gather in the crop, stems may need some coaxing into the tray as they are cut. Jenquip makes a similar machine with an infeed reel and elevator. If you can afford the greater purchase cost, these added features would be helpful. The *HT-KumaP c/w infeed reel* is shown in figure 36. The rotating reel sweeps material onto a wide conveyor belt. The collection bag is rather small and would quickly fill with stevia. George suggests replacing this bag with a lightweight trailer, perhaps with pushbike wheels. He also indicates they could make a higher mount for the infeed reel, at an ideal height for stevia plants.

Moving into a more expensive category, there are tractor-towed or self-propelled machines designed for cutting and gathering leafy crops like stevia. These are typically known as herb harvesters or harvester-mowers. This investment would only making sense when large areas are to be harvested. A single machine may be adapted to harvest many types of herbs or other similar crops. Multiple farmers might go together on a purchase and share a machine. In some areas, custom harvesting services or rental machines might be available.

From the Jenquip offerings, Merv George recommends their *HH2002C* range for harvesting large areas.[134] These are available in tractor-towed and self-propelled versions. They feature a bandsaw-type cutter and large conveyor. Various cutting widths are available, making them suitable for harvesting raised beds.

Some machines designed for cutting and gathering various crops might be adapted for harvesting stevia. Consider used machinery available in your area. At Canada's Southern Crop Protection and Food Research Centre in Delhi, Ontario, a tractor-towed, single-row peanut harvester was modified so that it was suitable for harvesting stevia.[135] It used a spinning cutter knife. A conveyor belt dropped harvested material into a peanut drying wagon. Additional cutters were added in order to cut plants into three pieces. This made the material flow more easily, avoiding the formation of large clumps.

Steve Marsden of Herbal Advantage Inc. describes one farmer's solution:

> The farm that grew Stevia for me for several years had a sickle mower with an elevator into a wagon being towed

---

[134] See photos and more about the HH2002C harvester at: http://www.jenquip.co.nz/herbharvesteHH.htm.

[135] Brandle, "Stevia," in *Richters Third Commercial Herb Growing*

behind. When the wagon was half full it was taken to the barn and an empty one was attached to the mower.[136]

Drying Stevia Leaves

High quality dried stevia leaves will be crisp and have a uniform, bright green color. Glycosides (including stevioside) are the sweet constituents in stevia leaves. Fortunately, these glycosides are not very sensitive to heat. But excessive temperatures may cause leaf discoloration.

Rapid drying produces the best leaf quality. Longer drying times will result in a lower stevioside content for the dried leaves. One source indicates "…the [stevia] leaf can be deteriorated by oxidation, losing up to 33% of the stevioside content after 3 days."[137]

Drying is accomplished with air movement and heat. According to Jim Brandle, stevia can be dried at temperatures up to 120°F (50°C), as long as the leaf is not burned, and it will remain stable.[138] The optimum drying temperature is about 110°F (43°C).

---

[136] Steve Marsden, personal correspondence, 2009.
[137] Rayaguru and Khan, "Post-harvest management of stevia leaves," 395.
[138] Brandle, "Stevia," in *Richters Third Commercial Herb Growing*

Figure 37: Dried stevia leaves on and off stems.

Stevia may be dried in the shade or in the sunshine. Some sources indicate sunshine will not degrade stevia leaf quality. However, one study found stevioside content was significantly less in stevia leaves dried by sunlight as compared to electric or gas-heated forced air.[139] Differing results may depend on the length of time leaves are exposed to sunlight. A thin layer (about 4 in. or 10 cm depth) of cut plant material can dry in 9–12 hours in bright sunshine with low humidity, while bulk kiln drying can take up to 2 days.[140]

Equipment and techniques for drying stevia could included the following:

- Indoor food dehydrators of various sizes
- Hang-drying upside down in bunches
- Large screens, nets, or perforated drying racks in buildings, greenhouses, or drying cabinets
- Bulk drying kilns (Building designed or modified for bulk forced hot air drying)
- Peanut-drying wagons (these use forced hot air)
- Alfalfa dryer

On a small scale, fresh leaves may be stripped from stems and dried in a stackable food dehydrator or on screens placed in a warm, dry location. Fresh leaves should be placed in layers less than about two inches (5 cm) deep. They will be ready for storage when crisp, breaking apart easily when crushed. Leaf moisture content should be 10% or less.

---

[139] Edilberto Princi Portugal, Giuliana C. Mercuri Quitério, Sylvio Luís Honório, "Influencia de fungos micorrizicos arbusculares... de Stevia rebaudiana (BERT.) Bertoni" ["Influence of arbuscular mycorrhizal fungi, cultivation systems and postharvest parameters in the concentration of steviosides and development of Stevia Rebaudiana (BERT.) Bertoni,"] Universidade Estadual de Campinas–UNICAMP (2006).

[140] Rayaguru and Khan, "Post-harvest management of stevia leaves," 395.

Figure 38: Dried stevia leaves in a food dehydrator.

Stevia leaves separate from stems more easily after drying, so this is the best approach when you have sufficient drying space. Hang-drying in bunches can save space. Gather together a few stems and bind at the stem base with a rubber band. Hang bunches upside down in a dry location. Something like twist ties or paper clips may be used as hangers when slipped under the rubber bands. Bunches may be hung from strings or ropes strung across the ceiling.

Another way to dry stevia leaves on stems is by spreading loosely in a layer no more than about six inches (15 cm) deep in a warm, dry location with good air movement. This could be in a greenhouse or other buildings. Fans or blowers can be used for air movement. The drying surface could be elevated nets or screens. The material should be protected from animals, pests, or any potential contamination sources.

Figure 39: Hang-drying stevia.

Plans are available for constructing small buildings or indoor drying cabinets with multiple drying shelves made of screen or perforated materials and with powered air circulation. Some models will add heat as well.

With larger production levels, bulk drying of leaves with stems is an option. Heated forced air is blown in from the bottom. This may be done in a peanut drying wagon, modified metal grain bin, or a bulk drying kiln (building designed for drying). The forced air must be allowed to escape out the top in some way. Depending on temperature, humidity, and air movement, the material to be dried may be stacked 2–3 feet (61–91 cm) deep and should be dry in 2–4 days. Stems tend to keep the mass open and porous enough that forced air will be able to infiltrate. In fact, the material was stomped down to fit in more material in Canadian bulk drying experiments.[141]

There are multiple ways to do bulk drying. A drying kiln or modified grain bin will typically have a perforated, raised floor. Stevia stems with leaves are removed from the transport wagon and stacked on this floor. Air heated by propane or natural gas is then blown under the perforated floor with electric blowers. Hot air is forced up through the material.

In order to minimize handling, harvested material may be dropped directly into large crates in the field.[142] These are similar to apple crates, but with perforated or screened bottoms. Crates are placed in a kiln for drying. In this case, the kiln does not necessarily need a raised, perforated floor. Rather, the crates are kept up off the floor so that hot air can be blown beneath them.

Use of a peanut drying wagon can minimize material handling even more.[143] The wagon is pulled behind or beside the harvester. Harvested material is dropped directly into the wagon. Air heated with propane or natural gas is then forced into the wagon with blowers designed for peanut drying. A tarp may be tied loosely over the top of the wagon so that forced air can still escape from under the tarp.[144] This will provide some protection from wet weather.

---

[141] See Columbus, "Stevia," in *Richters Second Conference*, 3–10.
[142] Ibid.
[143] Ibid.
[144] See photo of drying wagons in Brandle, "Stevia," in *Richters Third Commercial Herb Growing*

Finally, Steve Marsden of Herbal Advantage Inc. believes an Alfalfa dryer may work well for drying stevia on a large scale, with the temperature set at 10 degrees above ambient temperature.[145]

Separating Leaves from Stems

These are some possible techniques for separating leaf from stems, starting with the smallest-scale, least expensive method:

- Hand stripping
- Rubbing screen (for tea grade)
- Chicken plucker
- Modified threshing machines (grain combine or bean harvester)
- Specialized leaf separation machines

Usually, stevia leaves are dried on stems until completely dry (crispy and brittle, with 10% or less moisture content). But if you find too much leaf is pulverized or lost during the leaf separation process (especially with mechanized methods), it might help to do the separation before leaves are completely dry. In that case, leaves will need to be dried further after separation from stems. This could be done in a dehydrator with warm air circulation, or by spreading in a 2–4 in. (5–10 cm) layer on a clean concrete floor, tarp, nets, or screens in a dry building or greenhouse with good ventilation.

The goal of leaf separation is to end up with pure stevia leaves. Stevia stem tips may be included with leaves because

---

[145] Steve Marsden, personal correspondence, 2009.

they contain as much stevioside as do leaves.[146] Most leaf separation methods result in what is called "whole" dried leaf. In reality, the leaf will be broken up somewhat. At this stage it is ready for shipping or processing into tea grade or powdered leaf.

Hand stripping

Hand stripping is suitable for small quantities. When stripping by hand, start with complete stems that have not been chopped into sections. Hold 1–3 stems by the base with one hand and strip leaves with the other hand, starting from the base and working toward the tip. The stem tip may be broken off and included with the leaf. Gloves or a flower stem stripper can be helpful. I have used the *Flower Stripper*™ for hand stripping of dried stevia leaves.[147] It consists of a flexible plastic disk studded with plastic "pegs" on one side. Fold the pegged side loosely around the stem with one hand and pull down the length of the stem. With practice, you will discover the most effective technique. Strip over a container to catch the leaves. Multiple passes over stems may be needed.

Rubbing screen

In his book, *Herbal Harvest*, Greg Whitten describes a leaf separation method known as "rubbing."[148] It should work well for moderate quantities of stevia. It is generally used to produce a "tea grade" leaf. This consists of smaller particles suitable for herbal tea. Tea grade can also be further processed into powder.

---

[146] Rayaguru and Khan, "Post-harvest management of stevia leaves," 391.
[147] Available at floral supply outlets or try Wholesale Flowers & Supplies at http://www.flowersandsupplies.com.
[148] Whitten, *Herbal Harvest*, 199–209.

Rubbing by hand is done with a "rubbing screen" made of woven wire and attached to a wooden frame that contains the material being processed. Stems with leaves are stirred and "rubbed" by hand, separating leaves from stems. Leaf particles fall through the screen. Stems remain behind. The woven wire may be galvanized or stainless steel. Whitten recommends a tray size of a least 1100 x1800 mm, with an ideal mesh size being 1 mesh per cm and internal openings of about 8 mm for tea grade. The rubbing screen is fixed at about waste height, with two under-screens to catch stems that get through the rubbing screen. Under-screens should have larger openings, such as "chicken wire" or "bird wire" with openings about 13 mm across. Place under-screens so that material falls about 300 mm between screens. At the very bottom will be a catching tray to collect leaves. Even with under-screens, some stems may get through. Repeated screenings of the same material can remove more stem pieces. In *Herbal Harvest*, Whitten describes how to use and fine-tune this system for optimum results.

Chicken plucker

Another relatively inexpensive tool for leaf separation in moderate to large quantities is a traditional "chicken plucker" (or "picker"), normally used for removing feathers from poultry. This consists of a spinning cylinder studded with rubber "fingers." Bunches of whole stevia stems (not cut into sections) are held against the rotating cylinder. The "fingers" quickly beat leaves from stems. This idea comes from Steve Marsden of Herbal Advantage Inc. Marsden recommends doing leaf/stem separation before leaves are completely dry:

> Stem separation should be done when the Stevia leaves are 60% to 80% dried. Additional testing will have to be done to

determine the best dryness. If the leaves are too damp they will be hard to separate from the stem. If the leaves are too dry they will break up into small pieces. One way to do it is with a chicken plucker or a modified version of this is used to remove thorns from long stem roses.[149]

A chicken plucker can be purchased at a reasonable price. In 2010, the *Pickwick TTJ Table Top Picker* was available from Knase Co. Inc. for US $560 with motor or $360 without motor.[150] Powered stem strippers (normally used for cut flowers) might also work for stevia leaf separation. They use rubber "fingers" and work in a manner similar to a chicken plucker.

Modifying machines built for other crops

At Canada's Southern Crop Protection and Food Research Centre, a used grain combine was modified for stevia leaf separation.[151] Used in a stationary position, it "beats up" the dry material, knocking leaves from stems. The separated leaves come out where grain would normally come out.

In the question and answer section of the Richters Herbs web site, Richard Alan Miller suggests using a "bean harvester" for leaf separation.[152] In many farming areas, used threshing/harvesting machinery may be available that could be modified for stevia leaf separation.

Specialized leaf separation machines

Machines built specifically for separating leaves from stems are available mainly in Europe. They are quite expensive, but process huge quantities very quickly. These machines

---

[149] Steve Marsden, personal correspondence, 2009.
[150] See http://www.knasecoinc.com/pickers.html.
[151] Brandle, "Stevia," in *Richters Third Commercial Herb Growing*
[152] See Q&A section of http://www.richters.com (accessed July 2, 2010).

might make sense for large-scale herb farming or groups of farmers. Typically, spinning beaters dislodge leaf particles which then fall through a screen. Stems are ejected separately. Air movement and gravity may be used for separation as well. These machines might be listed as herb threshers, crushers, or separators.

Winnowing and screening

Some stem pieces may get into leaves during the separation process. Depending on the end use or market, you may need to process the leaves further to remove these stem pieces. This may be done by screening, winnowing, or a combination of each. A screen or "sieve" with properly sized openings will allow leaf through while excluding most stem pieces. Winnowing is done by allowing material to fall through an air stream produced by a fan. Heavier stem and dirt pieces fall nearly straight down while the leaves are blown to another location on a tarp or in a tray. Fan speed, distances, and technique can be adjusted for optimum results. Steve Marsden describes a method requiring only a fan, shovel, and clean floor or tarp: "Leaf-dirt separation," says Marsden, "we did by throwing snow shovels full of stevia leaves up against a four foot square fan. The dirt/sand landed right in front of the fan with the leaves several feet away."[153]

Contamination with soil

Dirt can get into stevia when rain or irrigation splashes the lower leaves or when cut stems are gathered by raking. Much of this contamination can be prevented by using mulch, raising the cutting height, and proper harvesting techniques. Contaminants such as soil tend to settle out. If soil is visible on

---

[153] Steve Marsden, personal correspondence, 2009.

tarps or at the bottom of bins or storage bags, it will need to be removed. This may be done by screening and winnowing. With screening, the sieve openings should be sized to retain most of the leaf while allowing the contaminants to pass through. Some fine leaf particles will be lost.

Leaf Storage and Shipping

Dried stevia leaves store well for at least two years as long they are kept in a dark, dry location. Dried stevia leaves are best stored in large plastic bags. For storing dried herb leaves, Greg Whitten recommends a 100 micron bag or double bagging with 50 micron bags. He recommends a bag size of 1000x600 mm for 5–8 kg of leaves.[154] Smaller bags may be used if you can't find the larger ones, but they will take longer to fill and move.

Clear plastic bags alone are usually adequate for dried leaf storage. For shipping, however, plastic bags must be placed inside some other container such as drums, strong cardboard boxes, or woven polypropylene outer bags.

Woven polypropylene bags will protect the inner clear plastic bags. Whitten recommends a bag size the same as the inner bag, and an outer bag thickness of at least 50 microns.[155] Woven polypropylene feed sacks are often available from feed and grain stores. Herb industry expert Richard Alan Miller recommends a portable, handheld bag stitcher (such as the Fischbein sewing systems) to close polypropylene bags.[156]

---

[154] Whitten, *Herbal Harvest*, 217.
[155] Ibid.
[156] Richard Alan Miller, *Herb Processing Facility 2002, Herb Farming Series Book 3* (Goodwood, Ontario, Canada: Richters Herbs, 2001) 19.

Steve Marsden of Herbal Advantage (a Missouri stevia leaf buyer) has the following to say about packaging and shipping stevia leaves:

> Some whole leaf Stevia is packed in compressed bales, jute bags, cardboard boxes with or without poly liners, and fiberboard drums. A lot of our Stevia is shipped directly to our grinder where some will be "cut & sifted." The balance will be powdered... We buy Stevia from all over the world. It might come into our warehouse by truck or by UPS depending upon the quantity. If a grower has several tons and is not too far away we pick it up in our own truck and trailer. When we were growing in Canada we found heavy duty boxes that were 4 ft x 4 ft x 4 ft with lids.[157]

Fiber drums may be purchased new, but Greg Whitten suggests obtaining second-hand drums with rubber-sealed, hoop-clamp lids. Drums that have been used for food products, says Whitten, are easy to clean.[158] Cardboard boxes are easy to find and stack compactly, but they are more susceptible to moisture and vermin. Boxes should be packed full to help prevent collapse when stacked with weight on top. Strapping may be needed for some boxes. No matter what bag, drum, or box is used, leaves should be stored up off the floor, such as on wooden pallets.

---

[157] Steve Marsden, personal correspondence, 2009.
[158] Whitten, *Herbal Harvest*, 217.

Chapter 6

Marketing and Economics

A stevia enterprise can take many forms. Depending on the laws and regulations in your area, products for sale may include:

- dried leaf
- fresh leaf
- tea grade leaf
- green stevia powder
- plants and seeds
- Stevia-related books

Larger volume sales might be made to various intermediaries such as:

- wholesalers (dried leaf)
- manufacturers/processors (dried leaf)
- herb shops and herbalists
- restaurants, grocery stores, and other retailers
- plant nurseries and greenhouses (plants)

Sales directly to gardeners and consumers might include all of the above products through outlets such as:

- on-farm sales
- mail order
- farmers' markets

The choice of stevia products and marketing outlets will depend on factors such as land availability, existing resources, expertise, current business model, labor availability, infrastructure, and location. Consider how stevia could work into your existing operation in terms of crop rotation, processing, and marketing. If you are already involved in field production of herbs or vegetables, for instance, it might make sense to add stevia to your crop rotation and market stevia leaves to your existing customers. If you already grow and sell bedding plants, you might add stevia plants to your offerings. If you grow and sell tea herbs or bulk herbs to wholesalers, stevia will fit right in. The idea of a super-sweet herb can grab the attention of potential customers.

Consider offering multiple products that appeal to the same customer base. If you already sell herbs to wholesalers, for instance, find out what other herbs they might need and grow those that fit your soil, climate, and production equipment. If you have a local or mail order clientele that enjoys your stevia leaf, you might also offer stevia books, seeds, and plants. This might mean purchasing some products for resale. If your expertise is in field production, you might offer stevia leaves from your farm and purchase plants, seeds, and books in bulk for resale to your customers as well.

Enterprise Budgeting

Careful planning will increase chances of success. Kansas State University has produced an excellent publication, available online for free, with guidelines and forms for developing your own herb enterprise budget.[159] *Farming a Few Acres of Herbs: An Herb Grower's Handbook* includes worksheets for calculating fixed costs, gross income, and profit/loss for several herb crops at a time. This publication also includes information about marketing and other aspects of herb farming. Download *Farming a Few Acres of Herbs: An Herb Grower's Handbook* at:

www.ksre.ksu.edu/library/hort2/s144.pdf

A 2005 article in the Journal *Current Science* includes a four-year budget for perennial stevia production in India, including yearly production cost and income estimates.[160] The article may be accessed online at:

www.ias.ac.in/currsci/mar102005/801.pdf

Another sample budget for stevia production in India was included in the November 2003 issue of the *Nabard Newsletter*, published by the National Bank for Agriculture and Rural Development.[161]

Selling Dried Leaves Wholesale

Wholesale markets for dried stevia leaves might include the following:
- manufacturers of products containing stevia

---

[159] Rhonda Janke, Jeanie DeArmond and David Coltrain, *Farming a Few Acres of Herbs: An Herb Grower's Handbook* (Kansas State University, 2005). http://www.ksre.ksu.edu/library/hort2/s144.pdf.

[160] Megeji et al., "Introducing Stevia rebaudiana," 803.

[161] Vinu Wadgaonkar, editor. "The Sweet Secrets of Stevia" in *Nabard Newsletter* 14, no. 8 (November 2003). http://www.nabard.org/newsletter/archive.asp.

- processors producing stevia extracts
- wholesalers and brokers
- herbalists
- herb shops and other retailers

Wholesalers and manufacturers/processors purchase large amounts of dried leaf and resell to others, sometimes after processing to various degrees. Herbalists, herb shops, and other retailers make smaller purchasers and typically sell to end users.

In the mid 1990's, Canadian researcher Mike Columbus estimated a dry leaf yield of 2200 kg/ha (1964 lb/acre) would be required to break even on stevia farming. But he was optimistic that improvements in agronomic practices, mechanization, and other factors would bring costs down.[162]

Marketing

Marketing efforts are important for profitability. It may be difficult for a new grower to secure purchasing contracts. But bulk buyers might tell you if they are looking for stevia leaves. Some buyers will be open to having dried leaves shipped to their location, even across international borders. A few potential buyers are listed in the appendix. Also consider contacting manufacturers of herbal teas and other herbal products. Stevia is becoming a common ingredient in many different medicinal and culinary herbal products.

Land requirement and quantity

Scale of field production will depend on land availability, requirements of buyers, and the capabilities of your equipment. About ¼ acre of production might be needed to meet

---

[162] Columbus, "The Cultivation of Stevia, Nature's Sweetener"

minimum purchasing requirements of some wholesalers, processors, and manufacturers. A quarter acre should usually yield at least 500 lb. dried leaves per year.

Very small plots will be sufficient for retail buyers and some wholesale buyers. Herbalists, herb shops, and other retailers will make purchases in much smaller quantities, and at higher prices. But marketing and packaging costs will be higher.

For the sake of crop rotation, risk management, and full utilization of machinery, you will probably want to grow other horticultural crops as well. Good crop choices might include vegetables or herbs that appeal to your customers and make best use of your soils, climate, and machinery.

Costs

The initial investment can be fairly small with a limited plot size and reliance on your own hand labor. With any new crop, it's always wise to start small and grow as you gain experience and customers. Labor-saving machinery can be added as production grows and proven markets develop.

In the mid 1990's, several Canadian farmers tried field production of stevia. Their production cost was about Can $8500 per hectare (Can $3441/acre).[163] This was without mulching. Weed control was a major cost item. Mulching might bring down overall costs by reducing irrigation and weeding costs. Mulching might also boost yields.

The various sections of this book will help in estimating your costs for some aspects of dried leaf production. Many cost items will be similar to other herb or vegetable cops. Local extension agents and university horticulture specialists can

---

[163] See Columbus, "Stevia," in *Richters Second Conference*, 3–10.

help you determine the cost of many these items in your region. Cost items might include:

- producing or purchasing plants
- transplanting to the field
- weed control
- irrigation
- soil tillage
- fertilization
- mulching
- low tunnel row covers
- harvesting
- drying
- leaf separation
- leaf storage

The largest essential cost (other than land) might be seeds or plants. Field trials by Kansas State University researchers employed one by two foot plant spacing, resulting in a planting density of 21,780 plants/acre.[164] This would mean 5445 plants for ¼ acre. Enough seeds to produce 5445 plants might cost aboutUS $290.[165] As described in chapter four, however, studies indicate higher yields should result from much higher planting densities such as 140,000 plants/ha (56,660/acre). This would be 14,165 plants per ¼ acre. For large-scale production in the mid 1990's, researchers in Canada estimated a cost of production for plugs from seed at Can 2.8¢–2.9¢ each.[166]

In cold-winter climates, a greenhouse and additional supplies would be needed for growing transplants. As production

---

[164] Janke, *Farming a Few Acres of Herbs: Stevia*

[165] Based on seed prices in 2010 from Prairie Oak Publishing, www.steviaseed.com. Seed numbers increased by 40% over plant numbers to account for losses.

[166] Brandle, "Stevia," in *Richters Third Commercial Herb Growing*

expands, investments in machinery for planting, tending, harvesting, and drying can go quite high. Renting and sharing equipment can keep costs down. Adapting used machinery to the job can cut costs as well.

Potential gross income

Prices (US dollars) for whole, powdered, or cut dried stevia leaf are listed below in figure 40. Per-pound prices were advertised on company web sites in the year 2010 and apply to a purchase of one or two pounds. Bulk wholesale pricing in larger amounts might typically be half of these retail prices (far right column). Company web sites and contact information are listed in appendix 3.

Supplier	Form	Price/ pound	½ of retail
San Francisco Herb Co.	cut & sifted	$6.40	$3.20
Mountain Rose Herbs	whole organic	$9.00	$4.50
Richters Herb Co.	cut	$21.31	$10.66
Frontier Natural Products Co-op	powdered organic	$19.80	$9.90
Jean's Greens	whole	$16.00	$8.00
Wild Weeds	cut & sifted organic	$22.25	$11.13
Herbal Advantage, Inc.	whole	$19.30	$9.65
Starwest Botanicals	cut & sifted organic	$18.92	$9.46

Figure 40: Advertised dried stevia leaf prices. *US dollars, year 2010.*

In the year 2002, Kansas State University researchers estimated a gross income potential of US $7686–$43,492 per acre for wholesale dried stevia leaves.[167] This was based on retail prices of US $6.50–$36.77 per pound and an annual yield of

---

[167] Janke, *Farming a Few Acres of Herbs: Stevia*

2365 lb/acre. A wholesale price estimate (about US $3.25–$18.39 per pound) was obtained by dividing retail prices in half.[168] Using these parameters, ¼ acre would yield about 591 lb. dry leaves, for a gross income of about US $1921–$10,873.

These yield results from Kansas State University partially derived from a non-irrigated crop in a dry climate. See Appendix 1 for yield results from field trials around the world. This will give you a rough idea of what to expect in your area. Many of the trials are small-scale and involve a small number of plants. Extrapolation is used for the "per acre" and "per hectare" yield data. These yields might be expected for intensively managed small-scale production under optimum conditions. Annual dry leaf yield results from small-scale trials include the following:

Annual Dry Leaf Yields From Small-Scale Trials

- 12,317 lb/acre (13,800 kg/ha) in West Java, Indonesia[169]
- 6945 lb/acre (7786 kg/ha) from seed at Giza, Egypt[170]
- 2081 lb/acre (2330 kg/ha) near Bonn, Germany[171]
- 2938 lb/acre (3290 kg/ha) at Bangalore, India[172]
- 2411–5867 lb/acre (2700–6570 kg/ha) near Pisa, Italy[173]
- 1454 lb/acre (1628 kg/ha) in first year and 2877 lb/acre (3222 kg/ha) in second year in Himachal Pradesh, India[174]

---

[168] For a list of stevia vendors with pricing, see Janke, DeArmond and Coltrain, *Farming a Few Acres of Herbs: An Herb Grower's Handbook,* page B10.

[169] Approximate yield with black plastic mulch and highest planting density. Perennial cycle. Basuki and Sumaryono, "Effect of black plastic mulch and plant density"

[170] Attia et al., "Effect of Propagation Method and Nitrogen"

[171] Annual cycle at 32,377 plants/acre (80,000/ha). Pude, Schmitz-Eiberger, and Noga, "Development, Yield"

[172] Chalapathi, Shivaraj, and Ramakrishana, "Nutrient uptake and yield of Stevia"

[173] Andolfi, Macchia, and Ceccarini, "Agronomic-productive"

[174] Perennial cycle with winter dormancy. Megeji et al., "Introducing Stevia rebaudiana," 803.

- 4849 lb/acre (5430 kg/ha) near Kiev, Ukraine.[175]

Yields in large-scale field production (a quarter acre or more) would typically be lower than for small-scale plots. Annual dry leaf yields from large-scale trials or farmer surveys include the following:

Annual Dry Leaf Yields From Large-Scale Trials

- 3285 lb/acre (3680 kg/ha) with irrigation in Kansas, US[176]
- 1964–2232 lb/acre (2200–2500 kg/ha) in Ontario, Canada[177]

A 2002 report concluded stevia has a good potential for profitability in parts of Australia. The authors estimate a possible gross income of AU $7500–$15,000 per hectare in Central Queensland.[178] The report concludes,

> Production should be possible in a number of locations provided irrigation water is available. As relatively small areas of Stevia are likely to be viable, it has potential to be an additional crop on existing farms. It could be added to vegetable production, tobacco, cotton, cane, pasture seed, lucerne or even dairy production. Coastal areas, with higher humidity and lower temperature extremes, are likely to be better suited than inland areas.[179]

---

[175] В.М. Завгородній [Zavgorodniy]; ОПТИМІЗАЦІЯ ЕЛЕМЕНТІВ ТЕХНОЛОГІЇ ВИРОЩУВАННЯ СТЕВІЇ В УМОВАХ ЛІСОСТЕПУ УКРАЇНИ. ІНСТИТУТ ЦУКРОВИХ БУРЯКІВ УКРАЇНСЬКОЇ АКАДЕМІЇ АГРАРНИХ НАУК. ["Optimization of Technology of Cultivation of Stevia Under Conditions of Steppes of Ukraine"]

[176] Annual cycle. Janke, *Farming a Few Acres of Herbs: Stevia*

[177] Annual cycle. Brandle, "Stevia," in *Richters Third Commercial Herb Growing*

[178] D. J. Midmore and Andrew H. Rank, *A new rural industry - stevia - to replace imported chemical sweeteners*, RIRDC Project, No. UCQ 16A. Barton, ACT: Rural Industries Research and Development Corporation (2002) 16.

[179] Ibid.

The advertised price range for stevia is quite broad. As stevia production grows, the market will stabilize and stevia will become more of a commodity. As with any commodity, there is the risk of worldwide overproduction and plummeting prices. I believe demand for stevia will grow for a long time, but leaf quality and consistency will become increasingly important. Certified organic stevia will usually bring a premium price as well. In 2009, Steve Marsden of Herbal Advantage Inc. (US) estimated farmers could get US $8 per pound for high quality certified organic dried stevia leaves.[180]

Selling Dried Leaves Retail

If you are already involved in retail sales, consider adding stevia leaves to your inventory. Many herb growers sell through both retail and wholesale outlets in order to spread risk and maximize profits. Wholesale customers purchase large quantities, but retail customers pay a higher price per unit.

Marketing

A marketing program might include writing newspaper articles and giving talks about stevia to local cooking or health clubs. Live plants, seeds, slide shows, brochures, and books can make presentations more interesting. Where allowed, free samples of fresh or dried stevia leaves could be offered. Put a few dried leaves (enough for brewing a cup of tea) in a small reclosable bag with a label on it including your web site and other contact information. If allowed, hand these out at your farm stand, farmers' markets, and at talks and presentations.

---

[180] Steve Marsden, personal correspondence, 2009.

Costs

Cost items will be similar to those listed in the wholesale dried leaf section above, but the initial investment can be smaller. It is easier to start small with retail marketing because you do not need to meet the minimum purchase requirements of wholesale buyers. In order to produce an equivalent net profit, production levels can be smaller than for wholesale markets. This typically means a smaller amount of land is used and more of the work could be done by hand, avoiding the cost of machinery. Costs per unit of leaf produced might be higher, but profit per unit of leaf could easily be higher.

Potential gross income

When selling dried leaves at retail (directly to the end user), income per unit of leaf will typically be at least double that of wholesale pricing. In 2010, prices advertised by eight stevia leaf suppliers ranged from US $6.40 to $22.25 per pound (see figure 40). When sold in smaller amounts (by the gram or ounce), prices are higher.

Selling Stevia Plants

Stevia is capturing the imaginations of gardeners. The idea of plucking and eating a sweet leaf right off the plant is intriguing. Gardeners can dry leaves for later use. They can also make their own green stevia powder by pulverizing dried leaves in a food processor.

Marketing

Connect with gardeners through on-farm sales, farmers' markets, internet, or mail order. If you enjoy sharing your passion for gardening, this approach might be good for you. Many gardeners will be sold on stevia with their first taste of a leaf. A marketing program for plants might include writing newspaper articles and giving talks on stevia to local gardening clubs or other interested groups. Live plants, seeds, slide shows, brochures, and books can make your presentations more interesting. *Growing and Using Stevia* is a small book that includes instructions for gardeners and 35 recipes using homegrown green stevia. It is available at a wholesale discount from Prairie Oak Publishing:

www.prairieoakpublishing.com

A similar approach might be used when marketing to nurseries, greenhouses, and other retail outlets. In this case, show your plants to the person in charge of plant purchases. Also have brochures or books available to tell the story of stevia and its uses.

If you have the skills and facilities for large-scale production of rooted cuttings or seed-grown plugs, consider marketing plants to farmers for field production. Serving this market requires great efficiency in order to bring down costs. Mail order plant sales are a possibility as well.

Costs

Cost items for stevia plants might include the following:

- greenhouse construction and operation
- seeds or plants
- pots and nursery flats
- growing media (potting soil)
- plant lights
- water and electricity
- pest and disease control
- skilled labor

In most climates, a heated greenhouse will be necessary. A small, relatively inexpensive greenhouse can get you started. You will need seeds, plugs (small plants), or mother plants from which to take cuttings. Seeds from Prairie Oak Publishing were US $188 per 5000 seeds in 2010. On a much larger scale, researchers in Canada estimated a cost of production for plugs from seed at Can 2.8¢–2.9¢ each in the mid 1990's.[181] Various seed and plant sources are listed in the appendix.

You can also purchase plugs and transplant them to bigger pots (typically 2.5–4 in. pots). Grow them for a few weeks before selling to your gardening customers. Plugs are small plants in "flats." Each plug occupies a separate small "cell" in the flat. Plugs can be grown from seed or stem cuttings. As an example, a flat of 100 plugs from Hillcrest Nursery went for US $54 in 2010 (54¢ per plug).[182]

Another propagation option involves taking cuttings from mother plants. Stevia stems strike root fairly easily, but this method requires more labor. Additional supplies would be needed, including pots and a growing medium. See chapter 2 for more on plant propagation.

Potential income

Stevia plants in three-inch pots would typically sell at a retail price (directly to gardeners) of US $3–$7 per plant in 2010. Wholesale prices (selling to nurseries, greenhouses, or other retailers) might be half of the retail price.

---

[181] Brandle, "Stevia," in *Richters Third Commercial Herb Growing*
[182] Hillcrest Nursery, http://www.herbcell.com.

Fresh Stevia Leaves

Most stevia leaves are used in the dry form. But people enjoy snacking on a fresh leaf when given the chance. Here are some ways to use fresh stevia leaves:

- **Garnish.** Fresh stevia leaves can be an attractive sweet garnish for cakes and other desserts, much like you would use fresh mint leaves. In fact, fresh stevia leaves could be combined with mint for garnishing.

- **Salads.** In small amounts, fresh stevia leaves may be used as a fresh green in salads, much like you would use curly cress or cilantro. Sweet stevia leaves add a unique flavor to salads.

- **Herbal Teas.** Fresh or dried stevia leaves may be used for brewing a fabulous herbal tea. A cup of tea requires a few leaves simmered in hot water. Stevia leaves blend nicely with other tea herbs such as mint.

- **Fruit Smoothies.** Several fresh stevia leaves may be added to the blender or food processor when blending a fruit smoothie. We usually include frozen bananas, other fruits, and a small amount of water or juice.

Marketing

If you already sell herbs or vegetables to upscale restaurants, try adding fresh stevia leaves to your offerings. Provide the chef with some of the suggestions listed above for using fresh stevia leaves.

Direct sales might be made to consumers at farmers markets or through Community Supported Agriculture (CSA) subscriptions. A small bag of fresh stevia leaves could be included in CSA shares. Make stevia a special feature by handing out flyers about using stevia leaves. Include tea recipes using stevia and other tea herbs. A small proportion of fresh stevia leaves could also be added to salad mixes or micro-greens.

Harvesting fresh stevia leaves

For fresh use, leaves should be clean and attractive. Consider cutting stems from the upper parts of the plant where leaves are more pristine. This usually means leaving 6–9 in. (15–23 cm) of stem behind. New branches will sprout from these stubs and from the plant crown. Pluck or strip fresh leaves from stems by hand. Stem tips may be included with leaves.

Fresh leaves may be harvested at any time, though younger stems may produce a more palatable leaf. Trials in the Czech Republic indicated the highest overall yield of stevioside (a sweet constituent of the leaf) in September. But the best yield of stevioside per gram of dried leaf was in July.[183] That is when fresh leaves probably had the sweetest taste. High rainfall in July that year may have played a role.

If you find good demand for fresh leaves, consider growing in a greenhouse when days are short. Use artificial lighting (such as a fluorescent shop light) left on 15 hr/day to prevent blossoming. This would make year-round stevia leaf production possible.

---

[183] Nepovim et al., "The effect of cultivation conditions"

Figure 41: Making green stevia powder in a food processor.

On-Farm Processing

The production of white stevia extract powder (an extract of one or more glycosides) is beyond the capabilities of most farmers. Very large output would be required to justify the start-up expense. The production of tea-grade or powdered green stevia is more feasible. But first check with officials about any regulations that might apply to this type of commercial processing in your area. In the US, a cooperative extension agent or USDA office might be helpful. With an effective marketing program, value-added processing can boost profits without the necessity of boosting leaf output.

Specialized machines can process large quantities of dried leaves. Small batch processing can be done with a normal kitchen food processor. Place dried stevia leaves the blender bowl and cover. A few pulses will result in particles suitable for tea bags. Additional time in the processor will create a green stevia powder that may be used in some recipes. Some powder will escape into the air. Keep covered for a while and consider wearing a dust mask.

For long-term storage, put green stevia powder in a glass jar with a tight lid and keep in a dark place. It stores at least two years this way without flavor loss. Short-term, green stevia powder may be stored in a strong, re-closeable plastic bag kept in a dark location. Stevia is often sold in plastic bags.

In general, 3–4 teaspoons of green stevia powder might replace a cup of refined sugar. It has unique flavor, so it will not work with all recipes. Customers will tend to embrace green stevia more readily if the have some good recipes to follow. *Growing and Using Stevia* is a small book that includes 35 recipes using green stevia powder or whole leaves. This book is available at a wholesale discount from Prairie Oak Publishing (see www.growingstevia.com).

Processing for added value could be as simple as packaging dried leaves in re-closeable plastic bags. Customers can use dried leaf "as is" for making their own herbal tea or they can make their own green stevia powder. *Growing and Using Stevia* includes instructions for making herbal tea and green stevia powder from dried stevia leaves.

Figure 42: Green stevia powder, whole leaf, and white extract.

Appendix 1

Field Trial Summaries

This appendix summarizes much of the stevia field trial data analyzed throughout the chapters of this book. Through the experiences of others, you can get a better sense of what to expect and what practices might work best. Trials can then be used to optimize a production system for your farm. All yields are per year.

The "Additional info" section of each listing indicates the scale, or size of the trial. For stevia, I consider about a quarter acre (.10 ha) or more to be large-scale production. In the case of small-scale trials, extrapolation is used to determine theoretical yields per acre or hectare. With real-world, large-scale conditions, yield per acre or hectare should be lower than the small-scale results suggest. But the lessons learned from these trials can often be applied to large-scale production.

Location: Near Delhi, Ontario, Canada (about lat 43°N)

Production cycle:	annual
Dry leaf yield:	2200–2500 kg/ha (1964–2232 lb/acre) [184]
Timeframe:	mid 1990's
Climate:	Continental. Cold winters. Hardiness zone 5[185]
Soil type:	Usually sandy, nutrient-poor[186]
Transplants:	Plugs from seed, 7-8 weeks in greenhouse[187]
Field preparation:	Plowing followed by discing and/or cultivating twice[188]
Field planting:	Early to mid May[189]
Planting density:	80,000–100,000 plants/ha (32,400–40,500/acre)[190]
Plant Spacing:	53 cm (21 in.) or 61 cm (24 in.) between rows. 20 cm (8 in.) in rows[191]
Fertilization:[192]	100 kg/ha (89 lb/acre) 6-24-24 before planting 140 kg/ha (125 lb/acre) urea, split application
Irrigation:	Frequent overhead irrigation — at least once per week during dry periods [193]

---

[184] Brandle, "Stevia," in *Richters Third Conference,* 158.
[185] See http://www.usna.usda.gov/Hardzone/hzm-ne1.html
[186] Brandle, "Stevia," in *Richters Third Conference,* 157.
[187] Columbus, "The Cultivation of Stevia, Nature's Sweetener"
[188] Ibid.
[189] Ibid.
[190] Brandle, "Stevia," in *Richters Third Conference* 157, and Columbus, "The Cultivation of Stevia, Nature's Sweetener"
[191] Columbus "Stevia," in *Richters Second Conference,* 6.
[192] Columbus, "The Cultivation of Stevia, Nature's Sweetener"
[193] Ibid.

Weed control:	Frequent tractor row cultivation combined with hand hoeing/weeding.[194] Unmulched
Pests:	Significant leaf damage from septoria disease (*Septoria steviae*), especially on over-mature plants. Some cutworm and deer damage[195]
Harvesting:	Mid to late September, just prior to blossoming using modified peanut harvester with conveyor that drops material into a wagon[196]
Drying:	Forced warm air (natural gas heat) in peanut drying wagons or kiln buildings.[197] 24–48 hr. drying time at 40°C–50°C (104°F –122°F)[198]
Leaf Separation:	With modified grain combine, stationary[199]
Dry leaf storage:	Cardboard boxes with plastic liners & strapping [200]
Production cost:	About Can $8500/ha (Can $3441/acre)[201]

Additional info.: Large-scale field trials conducted or coordinated by Agriculture and Agri-Food Canada's Southern Crop Protection and Food Research Centre. The stevia research team was headed by Jim Brandle. Several farmers participated on their own farms. Traditionally, this has been a tobacco-producing region.

Sources:
- Columbus, "The Cultivation of Stevia, Nature's Sweetener"
- Columbus "Stevia," in *Richters Second Conference*, 3–10.
- Brandle, "Stevia," in *Richters Third Conference*

---

[194] Ibid.
[195] Ibid.
[196] Ibid. and Brandle, "Stevia," in *Richters Third Commercial,* 158.
[197] Brandle, "Stevia," in *Richters Third Commercial,* 158-159 & Columbus, "Stevia," in *Richters Second Conference,* 7-8.
[198] Columbus, "The Cultivation of Stevia, Nature's Sweetener"
[199] Brandle, "Stevia," in *Richters Third Conference,* 159.
[200] Columbus, "The Cultivation of Stevia, Nature's Sweetener"
[201] Ibid.

- Jim Brandle, A.N. Starratt and M. Gijzen. "Stevia rebaudiana: Its biological, chemical and agricultural properties," Agriculture and Agri-Food Canada, Southern Crop Protection and Food Research Centre. http://www.lni.unipi.it/stevia/stevia/stevia0005.htm.

Locations: **Wichita, Kansas, US** (lat 37.6°N, irrigated)
Hayes, Kansas, US (lat 38.9°N, non-irrigated)

Variable tested: Irrigation. 72 g/plant dry leaf yield with irrigation. 32 g/plant without irrigation

Gross income: US $7686–$43,492 per acre. Rough estimate based on average estimated yield multiplied by ½ of lowest and highest retail prices found.[202]

Production cycle: Annual. Single harvest per year

Timeframe: 2000–2002

Climate: Continental. Cold winters. Hot, dry, windy summers
- Wichita: USDA Plant Hardiness Zone 6a. Average annual precipitation about 32 in[203]
- Hayes: USDA Plant Hardiness Zone 5b. Average annual precipitation about 23 in[204]

Planting density: 21,780 plants/acre (53,797/ha)
Plants surviving: 20,691/acre (51,107/ha)
1x2 ft. plant spacing

Dry leaf yield: Average: 2365 lb/acre (2650 kg/ha)
Irrigated: 3285 lb/acre (3680 kg/ha)
Non-irrigated: 1459 lb/acre (1635 kg/ha)

Additional info.: Large-scale field trials by Kansas State University

Source: Janke, *Farming a Few Acres of Herbs: Stevia.*

---

[202] For a list of stevia vendors with pricing, see Janke, DeArmond, and Coltrain, *Farming a Few Acres of Herbs: An Herb Grower's Handbook,* Page B10.
[203] Precipitation data from U.S. Dept. of Ag., based on years 1971–2000.
[204] Ibid.

Location:	**Davis, California, US** (lat 38.5°N)
Variables tested:	Planting density, position of stem cuttings, clipping height, frequency of harvesting, and productivity of clones
Dry matter yield:	Dry matter yield of 920 g/square meter with a single harvest at the end of the growing season.
Production cycle:	Perennial with winter dormancy. Top re-growth beginning in March.
Timeframe:	Two growing seasons, 1979–1981
Climate:	Temperate with mild winters and hot summers USDA Plant Hardiness Zone 9b
Transplants:	Successful rooting of stem cuttings in mist chamber four weeks at 70°F (21°C) with 10 seconds mist every 10 minutes. Cuttings from stem tips rooted most rapidly. Cuttings rooted in mixture of peat, sand, and fertilizer on 2x2 in. (51x51 mm) spacing. Fertilized with the following per cubic yard of mixed sand & peat: • 7.5 lb dolomitic lime • 2.5 lb hydrated lime • 2.5 lb single superphosphate • 1.5 lb urea • 3/8 lb of potassium sulfate • ¼ lb of 12-12-12
Planting density:	Optimum 16 plants/square yard in Yolo silt loam with no soil amendments.[205]
Pests:	Slugs damaged new spring shoots arising from over-wintered roots.

---

[205] Author's correspondence with Clinton C. Shock.

Harvesting: Best yield by harvesting once at end of growing season. Better plant survival from clipping at six-inch (15 cm) height rather than two inches (5 cm).

Additional info.: Small-scale field trials conducted by Clinton Shock at Davis, California (near Sacramento).

Source: Shock, "Experimental Cultivation of Rebaudi's Stevia"

Location: Chico, California, US (lat 39.7°N)

Variables tested:	Rebaudioside A levels over time and by harvest frequency
Production cycle:	Perennial with winter dormancy
Timeframe:	2001
Climate:	Hot, dry summers and cool, moist winters USDA Plant Hardiness Zone 9
Mulching:	"Poly ground cover" to conserve moisture and control weeds
Fertilization:	No significant differences in Rebaudioside A levels or biomass production resulting from different fertilization treatments.
Irrigation:	"Above ground drip irrigation works well"
Weed control:	"Poly ground cover"
Harvesting:	Maximum Rebaudioside A yield and optimum plant health resulted from multiple harvests per year as compared to a single harvest.

Additional info.: Small-scale field trials at California State University, Chico. The study found stevia is suitable for production in the Sacramento Valley and that "Rebaudioside A levels increase during the plants development before they again drop off as the plant reaches the flowering stage."

Source: Lau Ackerman (Principal Investigator), "Stevia as an Alternative Crop for Sacramento Valley Growers," CSU Agricultural Research Initiative (ARI) Final Report, 2001.

Location: Maryville, Missouri, US (lat 40.3°N)

Dry leaf yield:	26 g/plant (.92 oz.)
Production cycle:	annual
Timeframe:	2005–2010
Climate:	Continental. Hot summers. Cold winters. USDA Plant Hardiness Zone 5a
Soil type:	Heavy clay loam
Transplants:	From seed (started early march) or cuttings (started mid march)
Field preparation:	Permanent raised beds
Field planting:	Mid may. Mulched with straw.
Irrigation:	During dry periods
Pests:	Occasional aphids and whiteflies, but no significant damage
Harvesting:	September, when blossom buds first form
Drying:	Hang-drying bunches indoors. Takes 1–2 days
Leaf Separation:	By hand
Dry leaf storage:	In glass jars kept dark
Additional info.:	Small-scale trials by Jeffrey Goettemoeller.

Source: Personal observations of the author.

Location: Bangalore, India (lat 13°N)

Variable tested:	Fertilization levels and flat-top growing beds versus ridges and furrows
Dry leaf yield:	3290 kg/ha (2938 lb/acre) at a fertilization level of 60:30:45 kg NPK/ha (54:27:40 lb/acre)
Production cycle:	perennial
Timeframe:	Summer season of 1995
Climate:	tropical
Soil type:	Sandy clay loam. Alfisols. pH of 6.5. Medium availability of N, P, and K
Field preparation:	Slightly better yield with ridge and furrow method (2700 kg/ha or 2411 lb/acre) versus flat-top beds (2590 kg/ha or 2313 lb/acre).
Plant spacing:	45x22.5 cm (18x9 in.)
Fertilization:	Significantly better yield with 40:20:30 or 60:30:45 kg NPK/ha versus 20:10:15 or control. Entire fertilizer dose was incorporated into soil as a single application.
Harvesting:	Single harvest 100 days after transplanting to field
Additional info.:	Small-scale field trials conducted at G.K.V.K. University of Agricultural Sciences, Bangalore.

Source: Chalapathi, Shivaraj, Ramakrishana, "Nutrient uptake and yield of Stevia"

Location: Palampur, Himachal Pradesh, India (lat 32° N)

Variable tested:	Productivity of two different accessions
Dry leaf yield:	1628 kg/ha (1454 lb/acre) in first year and 3222 kg/ha (2877 lb/acre) in second year (accession 2)
Production cycle:	Perennial with winter dormancy. "With the onset of winter in November, growth of the plants ceased...Vigorous crop regeneration was observed during onset of spring (first week of March) from the underground root crowns" (page 802).
Timeframe:	2001–2003
Climate:	Sub-temperate humid. 1300 m above sea level
Soil type:	"...clay loam in texture, low in carbon (0.2%), high in total nitrogen (0.15%), medium in available P_2O_5 (0.18%) and available K_2O (1.48%), with a pH value of 5.6" (page 802)
Transplants:	Seeds sown July or February and transplanted to the field at 60 days old.
Field preparation:	"...field was irrigated prior to land preparation. Soil was thoroughly prepared by disc-ploughing, harrowing and planking" (page 802).
Planting density:	75,000 plants/ha (30,364/acre)
Plant spacing:	45x45 cm (18x18 in.)
Fertilization:	Well rotted farmyard manure thoroughly incorporated into soil at 25 tonnes/ha (22,325 lb/acre), 10 days before transplanting to field.
Irrigation:	Immediately after transplanting, 3 days after transplanting, and then every 2 weeks to a depth of 5 cm until arrival of winter rains

Weed control: Manually. Two hand-weedings and hoeings

Harvesting: Manually, two times per year (at flower bud initiation and again 90 days later). Stems cut 8–10 cm (3–4 in.) above ground level.

Production cost: "Cost of cultivation for producing an average leaf yield of 17, 20, 23 and 25 q/ha for first, second, third and fourth years respectively, was worked out to be Rs 4.74 lakhs/ha during four years."

Net returns: "Net returns for four years were calculated as Rs 3.75 lakhs, accounting for an average annual income of Rs 0.93 lakhs/ha at a sale price of Rs 100/kg dried leaves. It was, therefore, concluded that Stevia cultivation is a remunerative venture with a cost–benefit ratio at 1.89."

Using September 2010 currency conversions,[206] the average annual income would be US $1988.53 per ha ($805 per acre) at a sale price of US $2.14 per kg ($0.97 per lb.).

Additional info.: Small-scale field trials at the Institute of Himalayan Bioresource Technology, Palampur, India.

Source: Megeji et al., "Introducing Stevia rebaudiana," 801–804.

---

[206] Currency conversion done at http://coinmill.com, based on the International Monetary Fund conversion rate for the Indian Rupee on September 3, 2010.

Location: Greece (about lat 38°–41°N). Large-scale trials in 10 agricultural regions (Serres, Xanthi, Grevena, Katerini, Toumpa Kilkis, Lamia, Drama, Zagliveri, Tithorea, and Agrinio).

Variables tested:	"…adjustability, productivity and affordability" of stevia as a crop in Greece
Timeframe:	2006 and 2007
Climate:	Mediterranean, with mild winters and hot, dry summers. Predominately in plant hardiness zones 9 and 10 [207]
Additional info.:	Large-scale field trials. Studies conducted by the University of Thessaly.

> The plant's adjustability was proved to be satisfactory in conditions of limited fertilizer use and irrigation while is highly resistant to insects or diseases. Professor Lolas, who heads the University of Thessaly research program, stressed that Stevia rebaudiana can… lead consumers in Greece and the EU away from the use of sugar and synthetic sweeteners. The specific plant can ensure a good income for farmers even better than tobacco.

Source: "Experimental cultivation of stevia rebaudiana as alternative crop is 'promising'." 2010. http://www.grpressbeijing.com/english/read.php?id=3220.

---

[207] See zone map of Europe at: http://www.gardenweb.com/zones/europe/ (accessed July 2, 2010).

Location: State of Orissa, India (about lat 20°N)

Production cycle: Perennial

Climate: Tropical. Monsoon rains July–September[208]

Planting density: 40,000 plants/acre (98,800/ha)

Harvesting: First harvest 4–5 months after field planting, then harvested about every three months for up to three years after field planting.

Additional info.: Survey of stevia farmers in the state of Orissa, India

Source: Rayaguru and Khan, "Post-harvest management of stevia leaves," 395.

---

[208] See http://www.orissatourism.org/climate-in-orissa.html (accessed July 2, 2010).

Location: Sukabumi, West Java, Indonesia (about lat 7°S)

Variable tested:	Planting density and mulching. Highest yield with black plastic mulch and about 208,000 plants/ha (84,210/acre). Yield about 24% higher with mulch as compared to no mulch.
Dry leaf yield:	Highest was about 13,800 kg/ha (12,317 lb/acre)
Production cycle:	perennial
Climate:	Tropical. Air temperature 18°C–26°C. Altitude 950 m
Soil type:	Andosol sandy loam with 5% organic matter
Transplants:	Three-node stem cuttings rooted for 30 days
Planting density:	Best yield at about 208,000 plants/ha (84,210/acre). This is the highest planting density tried.

Fertilization: Incorporated before planting:
- Per m^2: 2 kg chicken manure and 11.33 g urea:TSP:ZK (1:1:1)
- Per ha: 20,000 kg chicken manure and 113.3 kg urea:TSP:ZK (1:1:1)
- Per acre: 17,851 lb. chicken manure & 101 lb. urea:TSP:ZK (1:1:1)

Applied after each harvest:
- Per plant: 1 g urea + 1 g TSP + 1 g ZK
- Per ha with 208,000 plants/ha:
  208 kg urea + 208 kg TSP + 208 kg ZK
- Per acre with 84,210 plants/acre:
  186 lbs urea + 186 lbs TSP + 186 lbs ZK

Weed control: Black plastic mulch significantly reduced weed growth and time needed for weeding.

Harvesting:	Every 1–2 months, when about 25% of the plant population was flowering. Cutting height of 15–20 cm (6–8 in.). Seven harvests in one year
Additional info.:	Small-scale field trials in randomized block design and three replications. Sponsored by the Bogor Research Institute for Estate Crops.

Source: Basuki and Sumaryono, "Effect of black plastic mulch and plant density"

Location: Okinawa, Japan (about lat 26°N)

Variables tested:	Fertilizer levels, planting density, seedling clone, and position of stem cuttings
Production cycle:	perennial
Climate:	tropical
Transplants:	From stem cuttings. Significantly higher first year yield with cuttings from stem tips as compared to other positions. Also large yield difference dependent on the clone from which the transplant was obtained.
Plant spacing:	First year dry leaf yield much higher per field area with 60x10 cm (24x4 in.) as compared to 60x20 cm (24x8 in.) spacing. Study authors suspect a smaller yield difference would be observed in subsequent years of a perennial cycle or with multiple harvests per year.
Harvesting:	Single harvest per year

Source: 村山, 盛一; 茅野, 良一; 宮里, 清松; 野瀬, 昭博; Murayama, Seiichi; Kayano, Ryoichi; Miyazato, Kiyomatsu; Nose, Akihiro. 1980. ステビアの栽培に関する研究: 第2報施肥量・栽植密度・挿穂部位および苗の栄養系が生育と収量に及ぼす影響(農学科); "Studies on the cultivation of Stevia rebaudiana BERTONI : II. Effects of the amount of fertilizer, planting density, position of the cutting and the seedling clone on growth and yield (Department of Agriculture)," *The Science Bulletin of the Faculty of Agriculture. University of the Ryukyus* no. 27 (1980): 1–8.

Location: Giza, Egypt (about lat 30°N)

Variable tested:	Propagation method (seed, tissue culture, & crown divisions) and nitrogen fertilization levels (0, 20, or 40 kg/feddan/cutting)
Dry leaf yield:	Highest was 4.39 tonnes/feddan (10,452 kg/ha or 9324 lb/acre) with propagation from crown divisions and 40 kg/feddan/year nitrogen fertilization. With propagation from seed, the total was 3.27 tonnes/feddan (7786 kg/ha or 6945 lb/acre).
Production cycle:	perennial
Timeframe:	Two experiments in two successive seasons: 2001–2002 and 2002–2003
Climate:	Very low precipitation. Hot summers. Mild winters
Soil:	Silt clay loam.

- 12.16% sand, 48.85% silt, and 38.99% clay
- pH of 8.10
- Available: 11.00 ppm N, 9.12 ppm P, & 35.86 ppm K.
- E.C. (mmohs/m3): 2.65
- CaCO3: 1.81%

Transplants:	Root divisions: Year-old plants divided into three parts. Replanted in field trial plots Tissue culture: Stem tip culturing Seeds: Variety *Spanti* planted in greenhouse. Transplanted to open field in 75 days
Field planting:	April 1
Planting density:	28,000 plants/feddan (66,667 plants/ha or 26,975 plants/acre)
Plant spacing:	50x30 cm (19.7x11.8 in.)

Fertilization:	Highest yield with urea fertilizer (46.5% nitrogen) at 40 kg/feddan/cutting (95 kg/ha/cutting or 85 lb/acre/cutting). First application of 40 kg/feddan at beginning of growing season in two doses, before first and second irrigations. After each cutting, the application was again made in two doses before irrigations.
Irrigation:	Irrigated as needed
Weed control:	manual hoeing
Harvesting:	Five cuttings/year: July 1, October 1, December 1, February 1, and April 1

Additional info.: Small-scale field trials at the Agricultural Research Center Experimental Station at Giza. Data are from the first year of production in both experiments.

Source: Attia et al., "Effect of Propagation Method and Nitrogen"

Location: Rheinbach, Germany (lat 50.6°N, near Bonn)

Variables tested: Planting density and plastic high tunnel treatments in 2002 season (25%–43% yield increase with plastic high tunnels). Fertilization treatments in 2003. Stem cutting rooting method in 2004–2006

Dry leaf yield: In 2002, best yield (5170 kg/ha or 4616 lb/acre) obtained with 140,000 plants/ha (56,660/acre) using high tunnel. Lowest yield that year (2330 kg/ha or 2080 lb/acre) obtained without high tunnel and at the lowest planting density (80,000 plants/ha or 32,377 plants/acre).

In 2003, stable manure fertilization produced highest dry leaf yield (6110 kg/ha or 5456 lb/acre). Trials in 2003 were in the open field with 110,000 plants/ha (44,519/acre).

Production cycle: annual

Timeframe: 2002–2006

Climate: Temperate Atlantic climate. Warm summers. Cool winters. Precipitation during 2002 growing period was 140 mm, with climatic conditions close to normal. The 2003 growing season was abnormally hot and dry, comparable to conditions of Southern Europe.

Soils: Research Station: Sandy loam. pH 6.8–7.4. High nutrient levels. In 2002, Phosphate, Potassium, and Magnesium were at 22, 19, and 17 mg/100 g soil, respectively.

Farmland (2006 trials): Loamy sand.

	In 2006, yields were better on the famland (loamy sand) as compared to the research station (sandy loam).
Transplants:	From root cuttings in 2002–2004. Stem cutting trials began in 2004. In autumn, mother plants were dug from field and potted in 2.8-liter containers with a 1:1 mixture of sand and propagation substrate. Plants were kept over winter under 16 hours/day grow lamps. Stem cuttings were taken from these mother plants. Better field survival rate (95%) and leaf yield by rooting in Jiffy pots™ as compared to compressed soil blocks.
Field planting:	May 16, 2002 and May 8, 2003.
Planting density:	Three treatments in 2002: • 80,000 plants/ha (32,377/acre) • 110,000 plants/ha (44519/acre) • 140,000 plants/ha (56,660/acre) Best yield at highest planting density.
Fertilization:	In 2003, all fertilizer treatments except stable manure resulted in lower dry leaf yields as compared to control. Stable manure produced highest yield (4420 kg/ha or 3947 lb/acre). Control yielded 4170 kg/ha (3724 lb/acre). Stevioside and Rebaudioside A also highest with stable manure. Treatments as follows: • No fertilizer applied (control) • Calcium ammonium nitrate (KAS) (27% N; at 370 kg/ha) • Stable manure (3% N, 4% phosphorous, 6% potassium; at 3330 kg/ha or 2974 lb/acre)

- Agrobiosol (7% N, 2% phosphorous, 3% potassium; at 420 kg/ha)
- Potassium magnesia (KMg) (30% potassium, 10% magnesium; at 560 kg/ha)
- KAS + KMg (27% N, 30% phosphorous, 10% magnesium; at 370 kg/ha KAS and 560 kg/ha KMg).

Preliminary results from trials in 2004 confirmed the advantage of stable manure for fertilization.

Diseases: After an unusually wet spring in 2005, leaf yield was impaired by *Sclerotinia spp.* infection.

Harvesting: September 3, 2002 and October 6, 2003.

Additional info.: Small-scale trials at the University of Bonn, Germany, Teaching and Research Station, Rheinbach. In 2006, trials were also done on farmland distant from the research station.

Sources:
- For trial years 2002–2004, see Pude, Schmitz-Eiberger, and Noga, "Development, Yield"
- For trial years 2002-2006, see Lankes and Pude, "Possibilities for Growth of European Stevia" in *Proceedings of the 2nd Stevia Symposium*

Location: Czech Republic (about lat 50°N)

Variables tested:	• Harvest timing. Highest yield of stevioside per plant (131 mg) in early September. • Propagation method (seed vs. stem cuttings). Stevioside content did not depend on propagation method.
Production cycle:	annual
Timeframe:	1996
Climate:	Temperate. Cold winters. Cool summers. Plant hardiness zone 5 or 6 [209]
Field planting:	June 5
Drying:	Leaf dried at 60°C
Additional info.:	Small-scale trial under field conditions

Source: Nepovim et al., "The effect of cultivation conditions"

---

[209] See zone map at http://www.gardenweb.com/zones/europe/ (accessed July 2, 2010

Location: San Piero a Grado, Italy (near Pisa, lat 43.7°N)

Variable tested:	Number of cuttings per year, propagation method, and winter hardiness
Dry leaf yield:	Ranging from about 60 g/plant in first year to 146 g/plant in fifth and sixth years. At 45,000 plants/ha, this would produce a yield of 2700–6570 kg/ha (2411–5867 lb/acre).
Production cycle:	Perennial with winter dormancy. Yields deemed economically profitable through fifth or sixth year.
Timeframe:	1992–2000
Climate:	Mediterranean. Hot summers. Cool winters. Plant hardiness zone 9 [210]
Soil type:	Silt loam. Sand 15.5%; silt 65.5%; clay 18.0 %; organic matter 1.15%; pH 8.1. Shallow water table
Transplants:	From seed and vegetative propagation
Field planting:	May 1992
Planting density:	4.5 plants/m² (45,000/ha or 18,219/acre) in 1992.
Fertilization:	100 kg/ha each of nitrogen, phosphorous and potassium, repeated every year at the end of winter. "The quantity of nitrogen distributed was always divided into two equal parts, one of which was used for winter fertilization and the other was applied immediately after resumption of growth by the plants (April)."

---

[210] See zone map at http://www.uk.gardenweb.com/forums/zones/hze6.html (accessed July 2, 2010).

Irrigation: Watered several times right after transplanting to help establish new plants. Later, irrigation done only during periods of low rainfall.

Harvesting: Dry leaf yield was greater with two cuttings/year (83.6 g/plant) as compared to single cutting/year (72 g/plant).

Additional info.: Small-scale field trials conducted by the Department of Agronomy and Agroecosystem Management at the Rottaia Agricultural Center in San Piero a Grado.

Source: Andolfi, Macchia, and Ceccarini, "Agronomic-productive"

Location: Kiev (Kyiv), Ukraine (about lat 50°N)

Variable tested:	Planting density, pruning (pinching), and mulching
Dry leaf yield:	5430 kg/ha (4849 lb/acre) with black plastic film mulch and planting density of 80,000 plants/ha
Glycoside yield:	435 kg/ha (388 lb/acre)
Timeframe:	2001–2003
Climate:	Continental humid. Warm summers. Cold winters
Mulching:	Mulching with black plastic film increased dry leaf yield by 2670 kg/ha (2384 lb/acre) as compared to control.
Planting density:	Best dry leaf yield and economic returns at 80,000 plants/ha (32,389/acre) as compared to 65,000 or 110,000 plants/ha.
Plant spacing:	Optimal spacing found to be 35x35 cm (13.8x13.8 in.).
Pruning:	Optimum time for plant pinching (pruning stem tips) was determined to be 35 days after transplanting to field (at the beginning of intensive growth). This treatment increased dry leaf yield by 2150 kg/ha (1920 lb/acre) as compared to control.
Additional info.:	Small-scale trials. Dissertation for degree, The Institute for sugar beet of the Ukrainian Academy of Agrarian Sciences.

Source: В.М. Завгородній [Zavgorodniy]; Источник: Автореф. дис... канд. с.-г. наук: 06.01.09 /; Ін-т цукр. буряків УААН.—К., 2006.—20 с.—укр. ОПТИМІЗАЦІЯ ЕЛЕМЕНТІВ ТЕХНОЛОГІЇ ВИРОЩУВАННЯ СТЕВІЇ В УМОВАХ ЛІСОСТЕПУ УКРАЇНИ. ІНСТИТУТ ЦУКРОВИХ БУРЯКІВ УКРАЇНСЬКОЇ АКАДЕМІЇ АГРАРНИХ НАУК. ["Optimization of Technology of Cultivation of Stevia Under Conditions of Steppes of Ukraine"]

Appendix 2

Stevia Leaf Buyers

Many herb brokers, wholesalers, retailers, and herbal tea manufacturers might be interested in quality dried stevia leaves, powdered leaf, or tea-cut leaf. Listed below are some potential buyers with a special interest in stevia.

JG Group/Stevia Canada Attn: Jonathan Gross
608 Pinedale Ave; Burlington Ontario L7L3W4 Canada
Phone: +1 (905) 634-8976
Web sites: www.steviacanada.com or www.JGGroupStevia.com
Email: info@SteviaCanada.Com or info@JGGroupStevia.com
Worldwide buyer of cut & sifted dry leaf and powdered dry stevia leaf, both certified organic and non-certified. Also a vendor of stevia seeds.
   "JG Group partnered with Stevia Canada is a Canadian leader in stevia manufacturing, production and distribution."

GLG Life Tech Corporation
999 Canada Place, Suite 519; Vancouver, B.C. V6C 3E1 Canada
Phone: +1 604.641.1368 Email: info@glglifetech.com
Buyer of whole dried stevia leaf, both certified organic and non-certified.
   "GLG Life Tech Corporation (TSX:GLG) is a world leader in the production of high quality stevia extracts including rebiana RA 97+. Our vertically integrated operations include stevia seed breeding, propagation, growth and harvest, extraction, refining and formulation. We provide customers in the food and beverage industry with the highest quality stevia available on the market today. Our goal is to improve wellness for consumers around the globe through innovative thinking and uniquely healthy products."

Herbal Advantage, Inc. Attn: Steve Marsden
131 Bobwhite Rd.; Rogersville MO 65742; USA.
Phone: (417) 753-4000 Toll free: (800) 753-9199
Web site: www.herbaladvantage.com Email: info@herbaladvantage.com
Worldwide buyer of dried stevia leaf in bulk, both certified organic and non-certified. Leaves would be transported by UPS or truck, depending on quantity. Herbal Advantage is also a grower and vendor of stevia plugs (flats of small plants) and larger plants, as well as herbal business supplies.

Sun Fruits Ltd. Attn: Shivraj Bhosle
11 Hanuman co operative society, Pashan Sus, Road, Pune, 411021-INDIA. Phone: 0091 20 25870624, Fax: 0091 20 25871525
website: www.sunfruit.biz Email: info@sunfruit.biz
Worldwide buyer of dried stevia leaf in bulk, both certified organic and non-certified. Interested in more than ten tons as a single consignment. Sun Fruits Ltd. is also a vendor of stevia plants and seeds. Mr. Bhosle adds:

"Sun Fruits Ltd has pioneered and perfected Stevia cultivation in semi tropical and tropical conditions. Sun fruits has developed semi perennial Stevia varieties that develop strong bushy growth & have multiple harvest possibilities and best organoleptic characteristics... Stevia is a natural choice for sweet flavour as a substitute for sugar and other synthetic and semi synthetic sweeteners."

Green Valley Stevia Attn: Inderpreet Singh Chawla or Rajpaul Singh Gandhi
Phone: 0091 9781 760 700 / 9814 060 700
Web sites: www.greenvalleystevia.com or www.greenvalleyfarm.in
Email: info@greenvalleystevia.com
Buyer of whole dried stevia leaf, powdered leaf, both certified organic and non-certified, from India and China. Minimum quantity of 50 MT per month. Green Valley Stevia provides both plants and seeds.

"Green Valley Stevia has set up an integrated supply chain of Stevia production in India, starting from cultivation through production and distribution of the final Stevia extract according to customer specifications of purity. With extensive experience in growing Stevia, a wide cultivation base, and a patented, chemical-free water based extraction technology, Green Valley Stevia is uniquely placed to meet the upcoming demand for quality Stevia extract at various purity specifications."

Steviva Brands, Inc.
725 NW Flanders St., Suite 402; Portland, OR 97209; USA
Phone: 1-(800)-851-6314
Web site: www.steviva.com Email: info@steviva.com
Buyer of dried stevia leaf in bulk.

Appendix 3

Selected Resources

These are just some of the places to go for information, machinery, and supplies.

Organizations

European Stevia Center
http://bio.kuleuven.be/biofys/ESC/ESC.htm
Includes articles and references relating to the safety of stevia.

European Stevia Association
www.eustas.org

American Herbal Products Association
www.ahpa.org

International Herb Association
www.iherb.org

American Botanical Council
www.herbalgram.org

ATTRA - National Sustainable Agriculture Information Service
www.attra.org Phone: (800) 346-9140 (English) (800) 411-3222 (Español)
Valuable collection of reports on a wide variety of sustainable agriculture topics including herbs, fertilization, row covers, greenhouses, mulching, and irrigation. Search the web site or call for assistance.

Books

Farming a Few Acres of Herbs: An Herb Grower's Handbook. Authors Rhonda Janke, Jeanie DeArmond, and David Coltrain. Includes information on pricing, marketing, and budgeting. Includes stevia. Kansas State University, 2005. www.ksre.ksu.edu/ksherbs.

Growing and Using Stevia: The Sweet Leaf from Garden to Table with 35 Recipes. Authors Jeffrey Goettemoeller and Karen Lucke. 2008. For home gardeners. Recipes use home-grown stevia. Available in English, German, Polish, and Spanish language editions. Available for resale from Prairie Oak Publishing. See www.growingstevia.com.

Growing Your Herb Business. Author Bertha Reppert. 1994.

Herbal Harvest: Commercial Organic Production of Quality Dried Herbs. Author Greg Whitten. 2004. Thorough treatment of small to medium sized herb farming.

The Legal Guide For Direct Farm Marketing. Author Neil D. Hamilton. 1999. Available from Growing for Market (www.growingformarket.com), Acres USA (www.acresusa.com) or Back 40 Books (www.back40books.com).

Medicinal and Aromatic Crops: Harvesting, Drying, and Processing. Editors Serdar Öztekin and Milan Martinov. 2007. Mainly for large-scale production.

The Organic Farmer's Business Handbook: A Complete Guide to Managing Finances, Crops, and Staff-and Making a Profit. Author Richard Wiswall. 2009. Includes enterprise budgeting guides.

The Potential of Herbs as a Cash Crop. Author Richard Alan Miller. 1998. Covers herb production, harvesting, processing, and marketing.

Start Your Own Herb and Herbal Products Business. Authors Entrepreneur Press and Rob and Terry Adams. 2003. Mostly about the business aspects of herb farming and herbal businesses.

Stevia Rebaudiana: Nature's Sweet Secret. Author David Richard. 1999. Answers many questions about the history and properties of stevia.

Stevia Sweet Recipes: Sugar-Free—Naturally! Author Jeffrey Goettemoeller.1999. Recipes using mainly white stevia extract powder and some using green stevia powder. Available in English, German, and Spanish editions.

Sources for Stevia Plants and Seeds

Richters Herbs
357 Highway 47; Goodwood, ON L0C 1A0 Canada
Phone: +1.905.640.6677
Web site: www.richters.com.
- Stevia plugs (flats of small plants) and larger plants.

JG Group/Stevia Canada Attn: Jonathan Gross
608 Pinedale Ave; Burlington Ontario L7L3W4 Canada
Phone: +1 (905) 634-8976
Web sites: www.steviacanada.com or www.JGGroupStevia.com
Email: info@SteviaCanada.Com or info@JGGroupStevia.com
- Stevia seeds.

Herbal Advantage, Inc. Attn: Steve Marsden
131 Bobwhite Rd.; Rogersville MO 65742; USA.
Phone: (417) 753-4000 Toll free: (800) 753-9199
Web site: www.herbaladvantage.com Email: info@herbaladvantage.com
- Stevia plugs (flats of small plants) and larger plants
- Herbal business supplies.

The Grower's Exchange.
P.O. Box 14860; Richmond, VA 23221; USA (mailing address).
Phone: (804) 829-6201 Toll Free: (888) 829-6201
Web site: www.thegrowers-exchange.com
Email: info@thegrowers-exchange.com.
- Stevia plugs (flats of small plants).
Will grow custom stevia orders with advance notice.

Gilbertie's Herb Gardens
65 Adams Road; Easton CT 06612; USA.
Phone: 203 452-0913 Toll free: 800-US-HERBS
Web site: http://gilbertieswholesale.com.
- Stevia plugs (flats of small plants).
- finished four-inch pots from stem cuttings.
Certified organic.

Wind Hill Native Gardens
PO Box 789, Banks, OR 97106; USA.
Phone: (503) 324-6870 Email: nature@aracnet.com
- Stevia plants, wholesale.

Hillcrest Nursery
21029 Gunpowder Rd.; Millers MD 21102; USA
Phone: 410-239-7781 Toll free: 1-(800)-452-4032
Web site: www.herbcell.com Email: orders@HerbCell.com
- Stevia plugs (flats of small plants).

Allow lead time of twelve weeks for pre-booked orders.

Blooming Nursery
3839 SW Golf Course Road, Cornelius, OR 97113
Phone: 503-357-2904 Toll free: 800-257-0719
www.bloomingnursery.com Email: sales@bloomingnursery.com
- Stevia plugs (flats of small plants).

Jolly Farmer Products, Inc
56 Crabbe Road; Northampton, NB Canada E7N 1R6
US: P.O. Box 787; Houlton, Maine 04730; USA
Toll free: 800-695-8300
Web site: www.jollyfarmer.com Email: sales@jollyfarmer.com
- Stevia plugs (flats of small plants) from stem cuttings.

Fry Road Nursery
34989 Fry Road SE; Albany, OR 97322; USA
Phone: (541) 928-7038
Web site: www.fryroadnursery.com Email: ann@fryroadnursery.com
- Stevia plugs (flats of small plants).

Morgan County Seeds
18761 Kelsay Rd; Barnett, MO 65011-3009; USA
Phone: 573-378-2655
Web site: www.morgancountyseeds.com Email: errolahlers@juno.com
- Stevia seeds
- Farm supplies including transplanters, mulch layers, and mulch lifters.

Prairie Oak Publishing
221 S. Saunders St.; Maryville MO 64468; USA
Phone: (660)528-0768
Web sites: www.prairieoakpublishing.com or www.growingstevia.com
Email: prairieoakpub@gmail.com
- Stevia Seeds
- Stevia books. *Growing Stevia for Market* and *Growing and Using Stevia* available retail or wholesale.

Seedman.com
  3421 Bream St.; Gautier MS 39553; USA
  Web site: www.seedman.com/stevia.htm
  • Stevia seeds.

Johnny's Selected Seeds
  955 Benton Ave; Winslow ME 04901. Phone: (877) 564-6697
  Web site: www.johnnyseeds.com
  • Stevia seeds.
  • Farm supplies including organic fertilizers, organic pest and disease controls, row covers, seeding and planting supplies, growing media, heating mats irrigation supplies, and a scythe.

Vanashree Agrotech
  J-116, Megacentre, Magarpatta, Solapur Road, Hadapsar
  Pune - 411 028, Maharashtra, India
  Phone: +(91)-(20)-26995697 / 30473811 / 30473811
  Web site: www.vanashreeagrotech.com Email: aloe25@gmail.com
  • Stevia plants.
  • Consultancy service for stevia growers.

S.J. Herbals and Health Care
  21, Sai Jyothi, 2nd Cross, K. B. Halli Main Road, P and T Lay Out
  Bangalore - 560 086, Karnataka, India
  Phone: +(91)-(80)-23221514
  Web site: http://www.sjherbals.com Email: sjherbs@gmail.com
  • Stevia plants.

Jeevan Herbs & Agro Farms
  178, Keshav Ganj, Sagar (M.P.) – 470002 India
  Phone: +91-7582-233049, 249910, 248935
  Web site: www.jeevanherbs.com Email: sales@jeevanherbs.com
  • Stevia planting material.
  • Agricultural consulting services.

ASR Herbals
  71/2, 21st A Main, Marenahalli, JP Nagar II Phase, Bangalore 560078
  India. Phone: 080-26493204, 080-36023169
  Web site: www.asrherbals.com Email: stevier@asrherbals.com
  • Stevia planting material.
  • Consulting services for those who purchase planting material.

GLG Life Tech Corporation
999 Canada Place, Suite 519; Vancouver, B.C. V6C 3E1 Canada
Phone: +1 604.641.1368 Email: info@glglifetech.com
- Stevia seeds.

"Our vertically integrated operations include stevia seed breeding, propagation, growth and harvest, extraction, refining and formulation."

Sun Fruits Ltd. Attn: Shivraj Bhosle
11 Hanuman co operative society, Pashan Sus, Road, Pune, 411021-INIDA. Phone: 0091 20 25870624, Fax: 0091 20 25871525
website: www.sunfruit.biz Email: info@sunfruit.biz
- Stevia plants
- Stevia seeds.

"Sun fruits has developed semi perennial Stevia varieties that develop strong bushy growth & have multiple harvest possibilities and best organoleptic characteristics."

Green Valley Stevia Attn: Inderpreet Singh Chawla or Rajpaul Singh Gandhi
Phone: 0091 9781 760 700 / 9814 060 700
Web sites: www.greenvalleystevia.com or www.greenvalleyfarm.in
Email: info@greenvalleystevia.com
- Stevia plants
- Stevia seeds.

"Green Valley Stevia has set up an integrated supply chain of Stevia production in India, starting from cultivation through production and distribution of the final Stevia extract according to customer specifications of purity."

Stevia Leaf Testing and Extraction

ChromaDex™
10005 Muirlands Blvd; Suite G, First Floor; Irvine, CA 92618; USA.
Phone: (949) 419-0288
Web site: www.chromadex.com/Services/index.html
Email: sales@chromadex.com
Stevia leaf analysis, testing, process development. Testing and quality control for food and beverage products such as tea.

Navin Process Systems
6,Vaidehi Residency, MIT College Road, Rambaug Colony,
Kothrud, Pune - 411038, INDIA
Phone: + 91 – 20 – 25460214
Web site: www.napro.co.in/contact.html Email: info@napro.co.in
Manufacturer and vendor of a stevia extract manufacturing plant.

Machinery and Supplies for Stevia Production

Jenquip. Attn: Merv George
Reid Line East, RD 5; Feilding, 4775; New Zealand.
Phone: 6 323 6146
Web site: www.jenquip.co.nz. E-mail: Jenquip@clear.net.nz.
Herb harvester machines that could be used for harvesting stevia leaves. Distributors around the world.

Knase Co Inc. Attn: Tom Knase
808 Rice St Suite 2; St Paul, MN 55117.
Phone (651) 488-7744 Toll free 1-800-808-3335
Web site: www.KnaseCoInc.com Email: tom@knasecoinc.com.
Leaf Separation. Tabletop chicken plucker suitable for stripping stevia leaves from stems.

Schweiss Welding
PO Box 477; 502 E. Lincoln Ave.; Fairfax, MN 55332
Phone: (507) 426-7828
Web site: http://schweisswelding.com E-mail: info@schweisswelding.com
Leaf Separation. Schweiss Chicken Pluckers suitable for stripping stevia leaves from stems.

Whiz Strip
P.O. Box 321; Castaic, CA 91310; USA
Phone: (661) 702-1977
Web Site: www.whizstrip.com Email: info@whizstrip.com
Leaf Separation. Flower stem cleaning machine that should work for stripping stevia leaves from stems.

Morgan County Seeds
18761 Kelsay Rd; Barnett, MO 65011-3009; USA
Phone: 573-378-2655
Web site: www.morgancountyseeds.com Email: errolahlers@juno.com
Farm supplies including transplanters, mulch layers, and mulch lifters.

Holland Transplanter Co.
P.O. Box 1527; Holland MI; 49422-1527; USA
Phone: (616) 392-3579 Toll free: (800) 275-4482
Web site: www.transplanter.com
Mechanical transplanters, plastic mulch planters, plastic layers/bed shapers/drip tape layers.

Mechanical Transplanter Co.
1150 Central Ave.; Holland, MI 49423; USA
Phone: (616) 396-8738 Toll free: 1-(800) 757-5268
Web site: www.mechanicaltransplanter.com

Email: mtc@mechanicaltransplanter.com
Mechanical transplanters, plastic mulch planters, plastic layers/bed shapers/drip tape layers, tunnel layers, plastic, hoops, and drip tape.

Market Farm Implement
257 Fawn Hollow Road; Friedens, PA 15541; USA
Phone: (814)-443-1931
Web site: www.marketfarm.com
Machinery for horticultural crops, from tillage to planting to harvest.

Peerless Manufacturing Company
U.S. Highway 82 East; Shellman, Georgia 39886; USA
Sales: (229) 679-5353, Ext. 1 Toll Free: 1 (800) 225-4617
Web site: www.peerlessmfg.cc/batch_drying_curing.html
Email: sales@peerlessmfg.cc. Manufacturer of dryers and dryer wagons. Primarily meant for peanuts, but also mention herbs.

Harmony Farm Supply and Nursery
3244 HWY. 116 North; Sebastopol, CA 95472; USA
Phone: (707) 823-9125
Web site: www.harmonyfarm.com Email: info@harmonyfarm.com
Organic farm and garden supply. Irrigation systems, organic fertilizers, ecological pest controls, tools, horticultural supplies, lab services, and consultation services.

Peaceful Valley Farm and Garden Supply
P.O. Box 2209; Grass Valley, CA 95945; USA
Phone: (530) 272-4769 Orders: 1 (888) 784-1722.
Web site: www.groworganic.com
Vendor of farm and garden supplies. Natural pest control, organic fertilizers, irrigation supplies, compost, natural weed control, plant propagating supplies, season extenders, and row covers.

Johnny's Selected Seeds
955 Benton Ave; Winslow ME 04901. Phone: (877) 564-6697
Web site: www.johnnyseeds.com
Farm supplies including organic fertilizers, organic pest and disease controls, row covers, seeding and planting supplies, growing media, heating mats irrigation supplies, and a scythe.

Robert Marvel Plastic Mulch
2425 Horseshoe Pike (Rt. 322); Annville, PA 17003; USA
Phone: 717-838-0976 Toll free: 1-(800) 478-2214
Web site: www.robertmarvel.com Email: info@robertmarvel.com
Plastic mulch, row cover, mulch layers, transplanters, drip tape, drip irrigation equipment, and greenhouse cover.

Berry Hill Irrigation, Inc.
3744 Highway 58; Buffalo Junction, VA 24529; USA
Toll free: (800) 345-DRIP (3747) Local or outside the USA: 434-374-5555
Web site: www.berryhilldrip.com
Drip tape, micro tubing, mulch layers, water wheel transplanters, and plastic.

Rain-Flo Irrigation, LLC.
929 Reading Rd; East Earl, Pennsylvania 17519; USA
Phone: 717-445-3000 Web site: www.rainfloirrigation.com
Transplanters, plastic mulch layers, and irrigation equipment.

Dubois Agrinovation
478, Notre-Dame, Saint-Remi (Québec) Canada J0L 2L0
Toll free: (800) 667-6279 Web site: www.duboisag.com
Irrigation supplies, plastic mulch, mulch layers, transplanters, low tunnels, floating row covers, greenhouse supplies, and large plastic harvest bins that might be suitable for stevia leaves.

Premier Horticulture Inc.
127 South Fifth Street, #300; Quakertown , PA 18951; USA
Phone: (215) 529-1290 Sales: (800) 525-2553
Web site: www.premierhort.com/eProMix/index.htm
worldwide distributor locator:
www.premierhort.com/eProMix/Horticulture/fHorticulture.htm
Complete line of Pro-Mix growing media.

Sun Gro Horticulture, Inc.
200 Burrard Street, Suite 1200 Vancouver, British Columbia; Canada V7X 1T2
Phone: (US): (425) 641-7577
Web Site: www.sungro.com
Vendor of a complete line of growing media, including organic media.

Vermont Compost Company
1996 Main Street; Montpelier, VT 05602; USA
Phone: 802-223-6049
Web site: http://vermontcompost.com Email: sales@vermontcompost.com
Organic compost and growing media.

Seven Springs Farm
426 Jerry Lane NE; Check, VA 24072; USA
Phone: (540) 650-3554 Toll free: (800) 540-9181
Web site: www.7springsfarm.com
Dealer locator: www.7springsfarm.com/dealers.html
Vendor of organic farming and gardening supplies. Fertilizers, soil amendments, growing mixes, pest management, row covers, and greenhouse plastic.

Sources for Dried Stevia Leaf

San Francisco Herb Co.
250 14th Street; San Francisco, CA 94103; USA
Toll free: 800-227-4530
Web site: www.sfherb.com

Mountain Rose Herbs
PO Box 50220; Eugene, OR 97405; USA
Toll free: (800) 879-3337
Web site: www.mountainroseherbs.com

Richters Herbs
357 Highway 47; Goodwood, ON L0C 1A0 Canada
Phone: +1.905.640.6677
Web site: www.richters.com

Frontier Natural Products Co-op
PO Box 299; Norway, IA 52318; USA
Phone: (800) 669-3275
Web site: www.frontiercoop.com

Jean's Greens
1545 Columbia Turnpike; Schodack, NY 12033; USA
Phone: (518) 479-0471
Web site: www.jeansgreens.com

Wild Weeds
PO Box 1016; Blue Lake, CA 95525; USA
Toll free: (800) 553-9453
Web site: www.wildweeds.com

Herbal Advantage, Inc.
131 Bobwhite Road; Rogersville, Missouri, 65742; USA
Toll free: (800) 753-9199
Web site: www.herbaladvantage.com

Starwest Botanicals, Inc.
11253 Trade Center Drive; Rancho Cordova, CA 95742; USA
Toll free: 800-800-4372
Web site: www.starwest-botanicals.com

Glossary

aphids—Soft-bodied, sap-sucking insects from 1–5 mm long. They sometimes infest tender young stevia leaves and stems. Infestations are usually not serious outdoors. More often, aphids are a problem indoors or in greenhouses. Controlled by insecticidal soap or insect predators such as ladybugs or lacewings.

cell pack—A container for starting plants—usually small plastic pots or "cells" attached in a group. The most common size is a 6-pack. Twelve 6-packs fit in a standard nursery flat for a total of 72 plants. Nursery flats with cell packs are widely available at general merchandise stores or by mail order and are ideal for starting large numbers of stevia or other bedding plants.

compost—Decomposed organic matter that can be used as a soil amendment or growing medium. Often part of potting soil or seed starting mixes. Mixed into garden soil, improves soil structure and fertility. In some soils, good compost is the only fertilization necessary for successful stevia production.

critical day length— the photoperiod that triggers blossoming. For *Stevia rebaudiana*, this is usually about 13 hours. This means blossoming will be triggered when a plant is exposed to less than 13 hours of light per 24-hour period over several days. To put it another way, blossoming is triggered when the plants are exposed to 11 or more hours of continuous darkness per 24-hour period (a critical dark period of 11 hours).

crown—where shoots emerge from the root system of a plant.

crown division—Over time, a stevia plant sends up new shoots from the crown. Crown division is done by digging up a plant, dividing it into two or more plants, and replanting those now smaller plants. Some of the root system and one or more above-ground stems go with each new plant. Typically, you might get three divisions from a plant that is at least a year old.

cultivar—A genetic strain developed for cultivation.

cutting—A section of plant stem used for asexual propagation. Stevia cuttings produce roots when planted in a suitable growing medium.

dehydrator—Appliance with shelves or trays designed to dry herbs and other material using low heat and circulating air.

direct seeding—Planting directly in the ground outdoors. Not recommended for stevia because of the small size and high cost of seeds.

drip hose—Special water hose used for drip irrigation. Water weeps or drips slowly from emitters.

drip irrigation—A watering method that minimizes water use and prevents wetting of plant leaves by slowly dripping water from drip lines.

drying kiln— A building designed or modified for bulk forced hot air drying of leaves.

fish fertilizer—Fish-derived liquid or powder designed to provide major nutrients to plants. Useful for stevia grown in low fertility soils when used in a more dilute solution than usual.

genotype—A distinct genetic plant strain. Many plant characteristics are controlled or affected by genetics.

genus—A taxonomic category consisting of a group of plant species with similar characteristics. *Stevia* is a genus name.

Within this genus, only the *rebaudiana* species contains large amounts of sweet glycosides.

germination—Emergence from a period of dormancy. Seed germination is the beginning of a growth cycle for plants like stevia.

glycosides—A group of molecules in which the sugar part is bound to another part. Certain glycosides, stevioside and Rebaudioside A being the most prominent, are responsible for the sweet taste of stevia. Rebaudioside A is considered to have the best quality of taste. Some authors use the term "stevioside" to mean all the glycosides in the stevia plant collectively.

green manure—A plant being grown for the purpose of improving the soil rather than direct harvest.

greensand—A slow-release natural fertilizer formed in marine deposits. Supplies mainly potassium (potash) along with many trace minerals. It can be used in potting soil, as a soil conditioner, or as a top dressing.

green stevia powder—Powdered dry stevia leaf. This is easily made at home from dry leaves using a blender, food processor, or mortar and pestle. Useful in some types of recipes.

growth chamber—A small enclosure where variables such as temperature, light, and humidity can be closely controlled. Used for tissue culture, rooting cuttings, and starting seeds.

high tunnels—Plastic-covered hoops over the width of multiple growing beds or rows. The frame is usually permanent, while the plastic is replaced periodically. High tunnels are initially more expensive than low tunnels, but might be ideal for plant propagation or overwintering mother plants in some climates. Typically, people and tractors can work inside a high tunnel.

hot caps—Small individual covers for temporary protection of young plants in the field

insecticidal soap—Special soap designed to control certain pests such as aphids by a direct spray application.

last frost date—The average date of the last frost in the spring. Since stevia is sensitive to cold, it should not be put outdoors without protection until at least two weeks after your last frost date when the soil is warm.

leaf separation—Separating stevia leaves from stems.

loam—Soil consisting of sand, silt, and clay, usually with a lower proportion of clay. Ideal for many plants including stevia.

low tunnels—Usually consist of slitted plastic sheets over wire hoops covering the width of one growing bed. These are temporary structures, erected and removed each year.

marginal climate—Climate where winters are usually not quite suited for winter stevia growth, but may allow for perennial production with winter dormancy.

mother plant—Plant from which material is taken for propagating new plants. Stevia can be started easily from stem cuttings.

mulch—Material placed on top of the soil, usually to hold in moisture during hot, dry periods. Organic mulches such a straw, leaves, or grass clippings also keep the soil cooler, provide food for earthworms, and gradually enhance soil fertility.

nursery flat—Shallow container for holding young plants. Can be fitted with a clear dome for seed starting. The most common US size is about 11 in. (28 cm) wide and 21 in. (53 cm) long.

organic matter—Soil organic matter is plant and animal material that has decayed. Vital for optimum soil structure and fertility. Can be supplied by mulching with organic materials or incorporating compost into the soil.

over-wintering—Surviving through the winter season. Stevia is a tender perennial native to subtropical regions with mild winters. In cold climates, it usually needs to be brought indoors or otherwise protected from freezing temperatures over the winter. Artificial lighting helps as well.

pappus bristles—Tiny, stiff, hair-like appendages attached to stevia seeds. Usually removed by seed companies.

perennial plant—A plant that normally lives more than two growing seasons. Stevia is a tender perennial, meaning it generally cannot survive outdoors where temperatures drop below freezing. It can be grown like an annual, however, replanted each year.

perlite—A type of volcanic glass. Horticultural perlite is very light weight. It has been expanded and has the appearance of small white beads. It adds air spaces to potting and seed starting mixes and is a good ingredient for media to root plant cuttings.

Plant Hardiness Zones—Geographic zones based on winter temperatures.

photoperiod—The duration of a plant's exposure to light in every 24-hour period. A more common term for photoperiod is "day length." But the light need not come from the sun. Artificial lighting can be used to provide a particular photoperiod.

planting density—The number of plants per hectare, acre, or other area measurement.

plant propagation—The process of reproducing plants. Stevia is usually propagated by stem cuttings or seeds.

plugs—Transplants grown in small individual cells.

potting soil—A medium for growing plants in pots or other containers. Should have the proper balance of air space and water holding capacity along with the necessary nutrients.

pre-conditioning mother plants—Exposing mother plants to a photoperiod of about 15 hours over a few weeks or more to ensure vegetative growth and inhibit blossoming. This prepares the plants for taking propagation material such as stem cuttings.

pruning—Removing a portion of a plant. In the case of stevia, stem tips may be removed 1–3 times during the early part of the growth cycle. This promotes beneficial branching.

raised bed—Usually a 3–5 foot (1–1.5 meters) wide, flat-topped, raised growing surface. Good for growing stevia in areas where soil drains poorly or is heavy (high in clay content).

ridge till—"tillage system involving scalping and planting on ridges built during cultivation of the previous year's crop... Since the ridges are preserved and rows are planted in the same location each year, traffic may be controlled."[211]

rock phosphate—Rock with a high proportion of phosphate minerals. Phosphate is one of the macro-nutrients needed by plants and may be supplied by fertilizers derived from rock phosphate.

rubbing screen—A woven wire screen attached to a wooden frame. Used for leaf separation. Dried stems with dried leaves are rubbed over the wire surface. Broken leaf particles fall through while stems remain behind.

---

[211] Donald L. Pfost, "G1652, Ridge-Till Tips," University of Missouri Extension. http://extension.missouri.edu/publications/DisplayPub.aspx?P=G1652

short day plant—Plant that blossoms as day lengths shorten. Most *Stevia rebaudiana* genotypes fall under this category. Plants generally produce blossoms only when exposed to 11 or more hours of darkness in every 24 hour period. The long days of summer at high latitudes tend to suppress blossoming and encourage leaf production.

silica gel—A porous form of silica that can act as a desiccant (drying agent). Available as solid blue beads that turn pink when saturated. Can be dried out and re-used. Good for placing in a sealed jar with stevia seeds for long term storage.

steeping—Soaking something in a liquid. Steeping stevia leaves is part of the process for making stevia tea and stevia water extract.

stem rot—Fungal disease of plant stems and leaves. Encouraged by high humidity and cool temperatures.

Stevia—The genus name for a large group of plants and shrubs native to South and Central America. More commonly, the term is used for a particular species, *rebaudiana*, having a significant quantity of sweet glycosides.

stevia extract powder—A white or off-white powder consisting mainly of one or more of the glycosides from the *Stevia rebaudiana* plant.

stevioside—The most prominent glycoside found in *Stevia rebaudiana*. Some authors use this term when referring to all the glycosides found in stevia collectively.

sun exposure—An expression of how much direct sunlight strikes a plant. In most places, stevia thrives with full sun or with afternoon shade. During the summer in hot climates, additional shade may be beneficial.

tender perennial—A plant like stevia that generally survives more than two growing seasons, but only where temperatures remain mostly above freezing all year. Stevia can be treated as an annual (replanted every growing season) in colder climates.

tensiometer—Device for measuring soil moisture availability.

transplant—A young plant meant to be moved to a new growing location or the act of moving a plant to a new growing medium.

tissue culture, plant—Multiplying plants in a sterile environment from plant fragments. May be used to produce clones of a stevia plant.

USDA Plant Hardiness Zones—Geographic zones based on winter temperatures. First established by the US Department of Agriculture.

vermiculite—Mineral with a high cation exchange capacity. Horticultural vermiculite has been expanded and is light in weight. Useful for potting and seed starting mixes and a good covering for stevia seed germination.

viable—For seeds, this means having the capacity for germination under favorable conditions.

whiteflies—Tiny sap-sucking insects. They congregate mostly on the underside of leaves. Sometimes infest stevia, especially indoors. Control methods include insecticidal soap and predatory insects such as lacewings.

winter dormancy—Cessation of active above-ground growth while roots remain alive and ready to send up new shoots in the spring. Perennial production of stevia with winter dormancy is normal in stevia's native range and under cultivation in many areas.

Bibliography

Ackerman, Lau (Principal Investigator). "Stevia as an Alternative Crop for Sacramento Valley Growers." CSU Agricultural Research Initiative (ARI) Final Report, 2001.

Andolfi, Laura, Mario Macchia, and Lucia Ceccarini. "Agronomic-productive Characteristics of Two Genotype of Stevia Rebaudiana in Central Italy." *Ital. J. Agron. / Riv. Agron.* 1, no. 2 (2006): 257–263.

Attia, A. E., O. H. El-Bagoury, A. I. Allam, and A. M. A. Elghany. "Effect of Propagation Method and Nitrogen Fertilization on Stevia (Stevia Rebaudiana Bertoni) Yield and Quality in Egypt." *Egyptian Journal of Agricultural Research* 83, no. 3 (2005): 1269–1292.

Basuki, S. and Sumaryono. "Effect of black plastic mulch and plant density on the growth of weeds and stevia." *BIOTROP special publication 38*. 1990, 107–113.

Brandle, Jim. "Stevia." in Rita Berzins, Helen Snell, and Conrad Richter, eds. *Richters Third Commercial Herb Growing Conference*. Goodwood, Ontario: Richters, 1999. 155–160.

———, A.N. Starratt and M. Gijzen. "Stevia rebaudiana: Its biological, chemical and agricultural properties." Agriculture and Agri-Food Canada, Southern Crop Protection and Food Research Centre. http://www.lni.unipi.it/stevia/stevia/stevia0005.htm.

Carneiro, J. W. P., A. S. Muniz, and T. A. Guedes. "Greenhouse bedding plant production of Stevia rebaudiana (Bert) Bertoni." *Canadian Journal of Plant Science* 77, no. 3 (1997): 473–474.

ČERNÁ, Katarína. "Physiological changes in Stevia rebaudiana (Bertoni) leaves caused by root sphere conditions." *Journal of Central European Agriculture* 2, no. 1-2 (2001).

Chalapathi, M. V., S. Thimmegowda, N. D. Kumar, G. G. E. Rao, and K. Mallikarjuna. "Influence of length of cutting and growth regulators on vegetative propagation of Stevia (Stevia rebaudiana Bert.)." *Crop Research -HISAR*. 21 (2001): 53–56.

Chang, K. F., R. J. Howard, et al. "First report of stevia as a host of Sclerotinia sclerotiorum." *Plant Disease* 81, no. 3 (1997): 311.

Chatzivassilou, E. K., D. Peters, and P. Lolas. "Occurrence of Tomato spotted wilt virus in Stevia rebaudiana and Solanum tuberosum in Northern Greece." *Plant Disease -St Paul* 91 no. 9 (2007): 1205.

Clarkson, V.A. "Effect of Black Polyethylene mulch on soil and microclimate temperature and nitrate level." *Agron. J.* 52 (1960): 307–309.

Columbus, Mike. "The Cultivation of Stevia, Nature's Sweetener." OMAFRA Herb Series, 1997.
http://www.omafra.gov.on.ca/english/crops/facts/stevia.htm.

———. "Stevia." in Rita Berzins, Helen Snell, and Conrad Richter, eds., *Richters Second Commercial Herb Growing Conference.* Goodwood, Ontario: Richters, 1998. 3–10.

Das, Kuntal, Raman Dang, and T. N. Shivananda. "Effect of biofertilizers on the nutrient availability in soil in relation to growth, yield and yield attributes of Stevia rebaudiana." *Archives of Agronomy and Soil Science* 55, no. 4 (2009): 359–366.

Das, S. A. and others. "Evaluation of the Cariogenic Potential of the Intense Natural Sweeteners Stevioside and Rebaudioside A." *Caries Research* 26, no. 5 (1992): 363.

Day Lengths for Various Latitudes.
http://www.orchidculture.com/COD/daylength.html#40N.

Επιμέλεια: Αλίκη Φωτιάδου. "Κερδίζει έδαφος στη Θεσσαλία η καλλιέργεια της στέβιας." TAHYDROMOS, 2009. [Alice Fotiadou, ed. "Gaining ground in Thessaly growing Stevia"]

Farooqi, Azhar Ali and B. S. Sreeramu, *Cultivation of medicinal and aromatic crops.* Hyderabad: Universities Press, 2001.

Farrar, J. J., R. M. Davis, et al. "First report of Verticillium dahliae on stevia (Stevia rebaudiana) in North America." *Plant Disease* August 84, no. 8 (2000): 922.

Filho, Lima O. F. de and MALAVOLTA, E. "SINTOMAS DE DESORDENS NUTRICIONAIS EM ESTÉVIA Stevia rebaudiana (Bert.) Bertoni." ["Symptoms of Nutritional Disorders in Stevia (Stevia rebaudiana)"] *Scientia Agricola* 54, 1-2 (1997): 53-61.

Garibaldi, A, D Bertetti, P Pensa, and M L Gullino. "First Report of Gray Mold Caused by Botrytis cinerea on Stevia rebaudiana in Italy." *Plant Disease: an International Journal of Applied Plant Pathology* 93, no. 3 (2009): 318.

Goettemoeller, Jeffrey and Alejandro Ching. "Seed Germination in Stevia rebaudiana." in J. Janick, ed. *Perspectives on new crops and new uses* (Alexandria, VA: ASHS Press, 1999) 510–511.
http://www.hort.purdue.edu/newcrop/proceedings1999/v4-510.html.

Hegazi, A. "Plastic Mulching for Weed Control and Water Economy in Vineyards." *ISHS Acta Horticulturae 536: 14th International Synposium on Horticultural Economics,* 2000.

Hilal, Arafa A. and Mohamed A. Baiuomy. "First record of fungal diseases of stevia (Stevia rebaudiana Bertoni) in Egypt." *Egypt. J. Agric. Res.* 78, no. 4 (2000): 1435–1448.

Janke, Rhonda, Jeanie DeArmond and David Coltrain. *Farming a Few Acres of Herbs: An Herb Grower's Handbook.* Kansas State University, 2005. http://www.ksre.ksu.edu/ksherbs/

Janke, Rhonda. *Farming a Few Acres of Herbs: Stevia.* Kansas State University, 2004. http://www.ksre.ksu.edu/ksherbs/stevia.htm.

Kamalakannan, A., V. Valluvaparidasan, K. Chitra, E. Rajeswari, K. Salaheddin, D. Ladhalakshmi, and A. Chandrasekaran. "First report of root rot of stevia caused by Sclerotium rolfsii in India." *Plant Pathology* 56, no. 2 (2007): 350.

Lankes, Christa and R. Pude. "Possibilities for Growth of European Stevia in Temperate Zones." in Jan M.C. Geuns, ed. *Proceedings of the 2nd Stevia Symposium 2008.* Leuven, Belgium: Euprint ed., 2008, 103–115.

Lewis, W.H. "Early uses of Stevia rebaudiana (Asteraceae) leaves as a sweetener in Paraguay." *Economic Botany* 46 (1992): 336–337.

Li, Thomas S. C. *Medicinal Plants–Culture, Utilization and Phytopharmacology.* Lancaster, PA: Technomic Publishing, 2000).

Lovering, N. M. and R. D. Reeleder. "First report of Septoria steviae on Stevia (Stevia rebaudiana) in North America." *Plant Disease* 80, no. 8 (1996): 959.

Maiti, C. K., S. Sen, R. Acharya, and K. Acharya. "First report of Alternaria alternata causing leaf spot on Stevia rebaudiana." *Plant Pathology* 56, no. 4 (2007): 723.

McCaleb, Rob. "Controversial Products in the Natural Foods Market." The Herb Research Foundation: Herb Information Greenpaper. 1997. http://www.herbs.org/greenpapers/controv.html (accessed 7-29-2010).

Megeji, N. W., J. K. Kumar, V. Singh, V. K. Kaul, and P. S. Ahuja. "Introducing Stevia rebaudiana, a natural zero-calorie sweetener." *Current Science* 88, no. 5 (2005): 802.

Metivier, Jacques and Ana Maria Viana. "The Effect of Long and Short day Length upon the Growth of Whole Plants and the Level of Soluble Proteins, Sugars, and Stevioside in Leaves of Stevia rebaudiana Bert." *Journal of Experimental Botany* 30, no. 119 (1979) 1211–1222.

Midmore, D. J. and Andrew H. Rank. *A new rural industry - stevia - to replace imported chemical sweeteners*. RIRDC Project, No. UCQ 16A. Barton, ACT: Rural Industries Research and Development Corporation (2002) 16.

Miles, Carol. Lydia Garth, Madhu Sonde, and Martin Nicholson. "Searching for Alternatives to Plastic Mulch." Washington State Uuniversity Vancouver Research and Extension Unit, 2004.

Miller, Richard Alan. *Herb Processing Facility 2002, Herb Farming Series Book 3*, Goodwood, Ontario, Canada: Richters Herbs, 2001.

村山, 盛一; 茅野, 良一; 宮里, 清松; 野瀬, 昭博; Murayama, Seiichi; Kayano, Ryoichi; Miyazato, Kiyomatsu; Nose, Akihiro, テビアの栽培に関する研究: 第2報施肥量・栽植密度・挿穂部位および苗の栄養系が生育と収量に及ぼす影響(農学科); ["Studies on the cultivation of Stevia rebaudiana BERTONI : II. Effects of the amount of fertilizer, planting density, position of the cutting and the seedling clone on growth and yield (Department of Agriculture)"] *The Science Bulletin of the Faculty of Agriculture. University of the Ryukyus* 27 (1980): 1–8.

Nepovim, A., H. Drahosova, P. Valicek, and T. Vanek. "The effect of cultivation conditions on the content of stevioside in Stevia rebaudiana Bertoni plants cultivated in the Czech Republic." *Pharmaceutical and Pharmacological Letters* 8, no. 1 (1998): 19–21.

Pfost, Donald L. "G1652, Ridge-Till Tips." University of Missouri Extension. http://extension.missouri.edu/publications/DisplayPub.aspx?P=G1652

Portugal, Edilberto Princi, Giuliana C. Mercuri Quitério, Sylvio Luís Honório, "Influencia de fungos micorrizicos arbusculares, sistemas de cultivo e parametros pos-colheita na concentração de esteviosideos e desenvolvimento de Stevia rebaudiana (BERT.) Bertoni" ["Influence of arbuscular mycorrhizal fungi, cultivation systems and postharvest parameters in the concentration of steviosides and development of Stevia Rebaudiana (BERT.) Bertoni,"] Universidade Estadual de Campinas–UNICAMP (2006).

Pude, R., M. Schmitz-Eiberger, and G. Noga. "Development, Yield and Selected Contents of Stevia rebaudiana." *Zeitschrift Füur Arznei- & Gewuurzpflanzen* 10 (2005): 37–43.

Ramesh, K., V. Singh, and N. W. Megeji. "Cultivation of Stevia [Stevia rebaudiana (Bert.) Bertoni]: A Comprehensive Review." *Advances in Agronomy* 89 (2006): 151–152.

Rayaguru, Kalpana and K Khan Md. "Post-harvest management of stevia leaves: A review." *Journal of Food Science and Technology* 45, no.5 (2008): 395.

Sativa, S.M. and others. "Stevia rebaudiana—A Functional Component for Food Industry," *Journal of Human Ecology* 15, no. 4 (2004): 261–264.

Schonbeck, Mark W. "Weed Suppression and Labor Costs Associated with Organic, Plastic, and Paper Mulches in Small-Scale Vegetable Production." *Journal of Sustainable Agriculture* 13, no. 2 (1999): 13–33.

Schrader, Wayne L., Jose L. Aguiar, and Keith S. Mayberry. "Cucumber Production in California." Publication 8050, University of California Agriculture and Natural Resources, 2002. http://ucanr.org/freepubs/docs/8050.pdf.

Shapouri, Hosein and Michael Salassi. "The Economic Feasibility of Ethanol Production from Sugar in the United States." USDA (July 2006). http://www.usda.gov/oce/reports/energy/EthanolSugarFeasibilityReport3.pdf.

Shock, Clinton C. "Experimental Cultivation of Rebaudi's Stevia in California." *Agronomy Progress Report #122*, University of California, Davis Agricultural Experiment Station, April 1982.

———. "Rebaudi's Stevia: natural noncaloric Sweeteners." *California Agriculture,* September–October 1982.

Singh, S.D. and G.P. Rao. "Stevia: The Herbal Sugar of 21st Century." *Sugar Tech* 7, no. 1 (2005): 17–24.

Sullivan, Preston. "Overview of Cover Crops and Green Manures." ATTRA - National Sustainable Agriculture Information Service, ATTRA Publication #IP024, 2003. http://attra.ncat.org/attra-pub/covercrop.html.

Takahashi, Luciana, Elena Melges E José Walter P. Carneiro. "Desempenho Germinativo De Sementes De Stevia rebaudiana Bertoni Sob Diferentes Temperaturas." [Germination Performance of Stevia Seeds Under Different Temperatures] *Brazilian Journal of Seeds* 18, no. 1, 1996: 1–5.

United States National Arboretum. "Introduction to the USDA Plant Hardiness Zone Map." http://www.usna.usda.gov/Hardzone/index.html (accessed July 2, 2010).

Wadgaonkar, Vinu, ed. "The Sweet Secrets of Stevia" in *Nabard Newsletter* 14, no. 8 (November 2003). http://www.nabard.org/newsletter/archive.asp.

Watson, Elaine. "EFSA opinion paves way for EU approval of stevia-based sweeteners." Foodnavigator.com. April 14, 2010.

Whitten, Greg. *Herbal Harvest: Commercial Organic Production of Quality Dried Herbs, third edition.* Melbourne, Australia: Blooming Books, 2004.

Wilk, Phillip and Wendy Dingle, eds. *Proceedings of the 3rd National Herb, Native Foods and Essential Oils convention, workshops and farm visits 14th–16th August, 2003, Lismore, NSW.* RIRDC Publication No 04/059 Project No TA 023-36. Rural Industries Research and Development Corporation, 2004.

Zaidan, L.B.P., S.M.C.Dietrich, and G.M. Felippe, "Effect of photoperiod on flowering and stevioside content in plants of Stevia rebaudiana Bertoni," *Jap. J. Crop Sci.* 49 (1980): 569–574.

Завгородній, В.М. [Zavgorodniy]; Источник: Автореф. дис... канд. с.-г. наук: 06.01.09 /; Ін-т цукр. буряків УААН.—К., 2006.—20 с.—укр. ОПТИМІЗАЦІЯ ЕЛЕМЕНТІВ ТЕХНОЛОГІЇ ВИРОЩУВАННЯ СТЕВІЇ В УМОВАХ ЛІСОСТЕПУ УКРАЇНИ. ІНСТИТУТ ЦУКРОВИХ БУРЯКІВ УКРАЇНСЬКОЇ АКАДЕМІЇ АГРАРНИХ НАУК. ["Optimization of Technology of Cultivation of Stevia Under Conditions of Steppes of Ukraine"] http://disser.com.ua/contents/15348.html.

Index

A

acid, 1, 58
Agricultural Research Center Experimental Station, 37, 60, 159
Agrinio in Greece, 153
Agrobiosol, 59, 162
agronomic practices, 3, 57, 126
AKS Herbal Research and Land Development Centre, 13
alfisol, 63
alternaria, 89, 90, 92
Alternaria steviae, 92
American Botanical Council, 169
American Herbal Products Association, 169
andosol soils, 72
annual production cycle, 4, 7, **8**, 11, 16, 24, 33, 36, 49, 53, 60, 62, 68, 71, 79, 81–83, 93, 94, 96, 98, 105, 142, 145, 149, 160, 163
annual weed control, 76
artificial lighting, 15, 16, 40, 49, 137
asexual propagation, 4, 33–36, 39, 44–49, 51, 54, 88, 89, 135, 146, 155, 157, 160, 161, 163, 171, 172
Asia, 11
ASR Herbals, 173
Asteraceae, 3, 86, 91
ATTRA - National Sustainable Agriculture Information Service, 169
Austin, Texas, 11

average minimum temperature, 11, 12
AZO, 63
Azospirillum, 63

B

bag stitcher, 121
Bangalore, India, 62, 63, 130, 150, 173
bean harvester for harvesting leaves, 116, 119
bed shaper, 65, 175, 176
bed shaping, 65
bed width, 66
bedding plants, 39, 40, 88, 94, 100, 124, 128
beneficial insects, 88
Berry Hill Irrigation, Inc., 177
beverages, 1, 167, 174
Bhosle, Shivraj, 168, 174
biodegradable mulch, 71
biofertilizers, 63, 64
biofuels, 2
bioproducts, 2
black plastic mulch, 22, 28, 72, 73, 74–79, 96, 99, 130, 155, 156
black spot, 92
Blooming Nursery, 172
blossom buds, 16, 20, 24, 25, 27, 82, 104, 149
blossoming, 15, 17, 18, 20, 22, 24–26, 28, 40, 50, 72, 82, 84, 104, 105, 137, 143
Bonn, Germany, 9, 24, 60, 79, 81, 82, 93, 94, 96, 98, 130, 160
books, selling, 124
boron deficiency, 85

boron toxicity, 86
Botrytis cinerea, 90, 92
Brazil, 16, 28, 39, 42, 85
breeding through selection, 54
British Columbia, Canada, 90, 177
broad mites, 88, 89
Brownsville, Texas, 11
budgeting, 124, 125, 170
bulk drying, 114, 115
bulk herbs, 124
buyers, 34, 126, 127, 133, 167

C

calcium ammonium nitrate, 59, 161, 162
calcium deficiency, 85
California, 3, 11, 12, 21, 25, 46, 77, 80, 91, 105, 148
calories, 1
Canada, 7, 11, 26, 27, 35, 36, 39, 62, 78, 87, 90, 101, 105, 109, 115, 119, 121, 122, 126–128, 131, 135, 142–144, 167, 171, 172, 174, 177, 178
cardboard boxes for storing leaves, 121, 122, 143
catching scythe, 106
cell packs, 40–43, 45, 49, 100, 135
Central Queensland, Australia, 131
charcoal rot, 92
Chawla, Inderpreet Singh, 168, 174
chicken manure, 39, 155
chicken plucker for leaf separation, 116, 118, 119, 175
chicken wire, 106, 118
Chico, California, 148
ChromaDex™, 174
clay soils, 57, 60, 61, 64, 66, 69, 149, 151, 158, 164
climate, 3, 7, 9, 12–14, 21, 24, 25, 36, 49, 50, 55, 62, 64, 77, 79, 88, 93, 96, 124, 127, 130, 135, 142, 145, 146, 148–151, 153–155, 157, 158, 160, 163, 164, 166
cloning, 34
cold storage of stevia roots, 9, 51, 55
cold-winter climates, 10, 128
Columbus, Mike, 26, 62, 78, 101, 105, 126
Compositae, 3, 86
compost, 38, 41, 58, 60, 64, 70, 176, 177
continental climate, 11, 27, 142, 145, 149, 166
continental humid climate, 166
Coral Gables, Florida, 11
corn, 2, 3
corn syrup, 2
cover crop, 64
crates for drying, 115
critical dark period, 17
critical day length, 17
crop rotation, 86, 124, 127
crown division, 5, 33, 34, 36, 37, 52, **53**, 54, 158
crowns, 4, 5, 13–15, 33–37, 51–54, 84, 90, 91, 137, 151, 158
cultivar, 34, 35
cultivars, high Reb-A, 35
cultivars, seed-grown, 35
cutting and gathering, 104
cutting height, 28, 105, 120, 156
cuttings, rooting, 44
Czech Republic, 24, 35, 104, 137, 163

D

Dallas, Texas, 11
damping-off, 89
Davis, California, 3, 12, 88, 146, 147
day length, 7, 9, 14–24, 26, 27, 35, 49, 104
day length at various latitudes, 20
dehydrator, 112, 113, 116

delayed blossoming, 18, 28
Delhi, Ontario, Canada, 109, 142
Department of Agronomy and Agroecosystem Management, 165
desert, 21, 75
determining day length, 19
die-back of plants, 12, 13
dirt, 9, 25, 105, 120
discing, 60, 64, 65, 142
diseases, 12, 25, 33, 36, 42, 53, 54, 69, **86**, 87, **89**–92, 96, 105, 134, 143, 153, 162, 173, 176
diseases,
    black spot, 92
    charcoal rot, 92
    damping-off, 89
    gray mold, 89, 90
    leaf spot, 90
    powdery mildew, 89
    pythium, 89
    root rot, 89, 90
    southern blight, 92
    stem rot, 89, 91
    Tomato Spotted Wilt Virus, 89, 91
division of plants, 53, 54
dolomitic lime, 48, 146
dormant, 9, 10, 13, 14, 25, 51, 55
drainage, 45, 48, 64
Drama in Greece, 153
dried stevia leaves, 2, 74, 103, 110, 111, 113, 117, 121, 125, 129, 132, 136, 138, 139, 167
drip irrigation, 45, 49, 60, 65, 69, 70, 71, 148, 176
drying kiln, 112, 114, 115
drying leaves, 103–107, 109, **110**, 112–116, 128, 129, 143, 149, 163, 170, 176
drying temperature, 110
drying time, 110, 112, 115
drying wagon, 109, 112, 114, 115, 143

Dubois Agrinovation, 177

E

economics, 123
EFSA, 2
Egypt, 21, 22, 26, 37, 38, 58, 60, 62, 75, 87, 92, 130, 158
equator, 17, 19, 26, 27, 28, 49, 84, 104
Erysiphe cichoracearum DC, 89
ethanol, 2
Europe, 11, 21, 119, 153, 160
European Food Safety Authority, 2
European Stevia Association, 169
European Stevia Center, 1, 169
evaporation, 68, 75
extracts from stevia, 126, 167

F

Farming a Few Acres of Herbs, 125
feed sacks for storing leaves, 121
fertilization, 3, 22, 37, 38, 41, 42, 47, 48, 57, **58**–63, 70, 128, 142, 146, 148, 150, 151, 153, 155, 157, 158–162, 164, 169
fiber drums for storing leaves, 122
field location, 57
field size, 33
field tillage, 65
first fall freeze dates, 27
first-freeze dates, 23
flood irrigation, 68
Florida, 11
forced air drying, 112, 114, 115
freeze, 14, 22, 23
freeze-free date, 22
frequent cuttings, 28
fresh stevia leaves, harvesting, 137
fresh stevia leaves, selling, 136
Frontier Natural Products Co-op, 129, 178
fruit smoothies, 136

Fry Road Nursery, 172
fungicide, 36, 87
furrow irrigation, 68
Fusarium oxysporum, 92

G

Gainesville, Florida, 11
garnish, 136
genetic variation, 4, 34, 54
genetics, 34, 35, 54
genotype, 4, 13, 15, 17, 18, 27, 28, 34, 35, 82
George, Merv, 107, 109, 175
Georgia, 11, 176
Germany, 9, 24, 48, 58, 60, 79, 81, 82, 93, 94, 96–98, 130, 162
germination, seed, 5, 39–42
Giza, Egypt, 21, 26, 37, 60, 130, 158, 159
GLG Life Tech Corporation, 167, 174
glycoside content, 34
glycoside extract, 126, 167
glycosides, 1, 5, 16, 17, 24, 28, 33–35, 58, 65, 104, 110–112, 117, 137, 138, 148, 161, 163
grain reaper, 106
gray mold, 89, 90
Greece, 3, 91, 92, 153
green manure, 64
green stevia powder, 35, 123, 133, 138–140, 170
Green Valley Stevia, 168, 174
greensand, 64
Grevena in Greece, 153
gross income, 73, 74, 80, 82, 96, 125, 129, 131, 145
gross income estimates, 129, 133
Gross, Jonathan, 167, 171
growing beds, 9, 24, 27, 49, 57, 64–67, 70, 71, 77, 79, 80, 98, 100, 101, 109, 149, 150, 175, 176

growing media, 38, 39, 45, 47, 48, 52, 54, 89, 134, 135, 173, 176, 177
growing season, 3, 7, 17, 22, 24–26, 54, 60, 61, 68, 71, 77, 83, 97, 105, 146, 147, 159, 160
Growing and Using Stevia, 134, 139
growth chamber, 42

H

hand stripping of leaves, 116, 117
Hang-drying, 112–114, 149
hard freeze, 27
hardening off plants, 43
Harmony Farm Supply and Nursery, 176
harrowing, 65, 151
harvest timing above 15° latitude, 24
harvest timing below 15° latitude, 28
harvester-mowers, 109
harvesting leaves, 7, 24, 25, 27, 103, 104–109, 119, 120, 128, 129, 137, 143, 146–152, 154, 156, 157, 159, 162, 165, 170, 175
harvesting, mechanized, 105
Hawaii, 11
hay mulch, 70, 71, 76, 77, 78
Hayes, Kansas, 68, 145
heat mat, 42
hedge shears, 106
herb harvester, 106, 108, 109, 175
herb separators, 120
herb shops, 123, 126, 127
herb threshers, 120
Herbal Advantage, Inc., 38, 45, 46, 66, 89, 109, 116, 118, 122, 129, 132, 168, 171, 178
Herbal Harvest, 106, 117, 118
herbal tea, 35, 117, 126, 136, 139, 167

herbalists, 123, 126, 127
herbicides, 75, 77
high latitudes, 5, 21, 26, 105
high tunnels, 9, 10, 23, 24, 79, 80, 82, 93, 94, 96, 98, 160
high tunnels,
   cost, 80
   gross income increase, 80, 82
   yield increase, 80, 81, 82
Hillcrest Nursery, 135, 172
Holland Transplanter Co., 175
Honolulu, Hawaii, 11
horticultural oil, 88
hot caps, 24
Houston, Texas, 11
hydrated lime, 48, 146

I

income, 2, 73, 80, 95, 125, 129, 130, 133, 135, 152, 153
income estimates, 129, 133
income, gross, 73, 74, 80, 125, 129, 131
India, 9, 13, 47, 58, 62, 63, 66, 67, 90, 100, 125, 130, 150–152, 154, 168, 173, 174
Indonesia, 28, 72–74, 96, 99, 130, 155
insecticidal soap, 88, 89
International Herb Association, 169
irrigation, 2, 3, 27, 60, **68**, 69, 90, 95, 120, 127, 128, 131, 142, 145, 148, 149, 151, 153, 159, 165, 169, 173, 176, 177
irrigation,
   drip, 45, 49, 60, 65, **69**, 70, 71, 148, 176
   flood, 68
   furrow, 68
   overhead, 67, 68, 142
Italy, 12, 13, 25, 90, 130, 164

J

Japan, 47
Jeevan Herbs & Agro Farms, 173
Jenquip harvesters, 107, 108, 109, 175
JG Group/Stevia Canada, 167, 171
Jolly Farmer Products, Inc, 172

K

Kansas, 2, 66, 68, 124, 125, 128, 129, 130, 131, 145, 170
Kansas State University, 2, 68, 124, 125, 128–130, 145, 170
Karnataka, India, 63, 173
KAS, 59, 161, 162
Katerini in Greece, 153
Kiev (Kyiv), Ukraine, 75, 83, 131, 166
Kilkis in Greece, 153
KMg, 59, 162
Knase Co Inc., 175

L

labor, 9, 33, 53, 71, 76–78, 80, 83, 95, 103, 124, 127, 134, 135
lacewings, 88
ladybugs, 88
Lamia in Greece, 153
land requirement, 126
lathe house, 49
latitude, 16, 17, 19, 21, 23, 24, 26, 27, 28, 104
latitude, specific latitudes
   $13°N$, 62, 150
   $15°N$, 27, 63
   $20°N$, 9, 154
   $23°S$, 39
   $26°N$, 157
   $30°N$, 21, 26, 37, 60, 158
   $32° N$, 151
   $32°N$, 13
   $37.6°N$, 68, 145

38.5°N, 12, 146
38.9°N, 68, 145
39.7°N, 148
40.3°N, 149
40°N, 21, 23, 25
43.7°N, 12, 25, 164
43°N, 142
50.6°N, 24, 48, 60, 79, 81, 82, 93, 94, 96, 160
50°N, 24, 27, 75, 83, 104, 163, 166
7°S, 28, 72, 73, 74, 99, 155
layering, 5
leaching, 62, 70
leaf buds, 47
leaf discoloration, 110
leaf growth, 5, 15, 17, 20, 21, 26, 28, 40, 58
leaf prices, 129
leaf separation, 103, 116–119, 128
leaf separation with chicken plucker, 116, 118, 119, 175
leaf separation with rubbing screen, 116–118
leaf separation, hand stripping, 116, 117
leaf spot, 90
leaf storage, 104, 112, 121, 122, 128, 139, 143, 149
leaf yield, 2, 16, 24, 25, 26, 28, 36, 37, 38, 47, 49, 58, 60–63, 65, 73–75, 79, 82, 83, 93, 96, 98, 104, 105, 126, 130, 131, 142, 145, 149, 150–152, 155, 157, 158, 160–162, 164–166
leaves, description, 4
legume, 64
lettuce seeds, 5, 41
long-day, 15, 21, 25, 44
Louisiana, 2
low tunnels, 10, 23, 79, 80, 128, 177
low tunnels, cost, 80

M

Macrophomina phaseolina, 92
magnesium, 59, 85, 160, 162
magnesium deficiency, 85
mail order sales, 100, 124, 133
manufacturers, 123, 125–127, 167
manure, 39, 58, 59, 60, 63, 64, 151, 160–162
maps, 7, 8, 13, 19, 23, 153, 163, 164
marginal climates, 11, 14
Market Farm Implement, 176
marketing, 123–127, 132–134, 136, 138, 170
Marsden, Steve, 38, 45, 46, 66, 89, 109, 110, 116, 118–120, 122, 132, 168, 171
Maryville, Missouri, 23, 25, 149, 172
Mechanical Transplanter Co., 175
mechanization, 103, 107, 126
mechanized harvesting, 105
Mediterranean climate, 13, 21, 25, 153, 164
Mexico, 7
Miami, Florida, 11
mild winters, 21, 26
Minnesota, 27
Missouri, 9, 10, 23, 25, 88, 89, 122, 149, 178
misting, 41, 47
mites, 88
Montana, 27
Morgan County Seeds, 172, 175
mother plants, 34, 45, 48–51, 53, 54, 55, 79, 135, 161
mother plants, pre-conditioning, 49, 50
Mountain Rose Herbs, 129, 178
mulching, 9, 13, 14, 65, 68–78, 83, 97, 101, 120, 127, 128, 148, 155, 166, 169, 172, 175–177

mulch films, 65, 69, 70, 72–77, 130, 175–177
mulch, benefits, 70
mulch, biodegradable, 71
mulch, cost, 77
mulch, hay, 70, 71, 76–78
mulch, paper, 69, 71
mulch, plastic, 9, 22, 28, 65, 69–79, 83, 96, 99, 130, 148, 155, 156, 166, 175–177
mulch, shredded leaf, 70, 71
mulch, straw, 9, 14, 52, 70, 71, 75–78, 149
mulch, water savings, 75
mulch, weed control, 75, 76
mulch, white plastic, 74

N

Naples, Florida, 11
National Bank for Agriculture and Rural Development, 125
National Climatic Data Center, 23, 27
National Sustainable Agriculture Information Service, 64
natural gas heat, 115, 143
Navin Process Systems, 174
NCDC, 23, 27
nitrogen, 13, 22, 23, 26, 27, 37, 42, 47, 58–62, 64, 74, 85, 87, 91, 130, 144, 150, 151, 153, 158, 159, 161, 162, 164
nitrogen deficiency, 85
nitrogen-fixing, 64
North America, 8, 27, 91
North Dakota, 27
northern hemisphere, 21
nurseries, 100, 123, 134, 135
nursery flats, 40, 134
nutrient deficiencies, 85
nutrient toxicities, 86

O

Okinawa, Japan, 157
Ontario, Canada, 26, 36, 62, 90, 121, 131, 167, 171
organic, 5, 14, 36, 38, 41, 58, 60, 64, 69, 70–72, 75–78, 87, 106, 129, 132, 155, 164, 167, 168, 170, 171, 173, 176, 177
organic certification, 78
organic matter, 5, 58, 64, 72, 155, 164
Orissa, India, 9, 154
overhead irrigation, 67, 68, 142
overheating, 24
overproduction, 132

P

Palampur, Himachal Pradesh, India, 13, 151, 152
pallets, 122
paper mulch, 69, 71
pappus bristles, 39, 41
Paraguay, 4
Peaceful Valley Farm and Garden Supply, 176
peanut harvester, 106, 109, 143
peas, 64
peat, 38, 41, 45, 48, 146
Peerless Manufacturing Company, 176
perennial production cycle, 7–14, 17, 25, 28, 33, 36, 49, 53, 60, 71, 73, 74, 76, 83, 96, 99, 125, 130, 146, 148, 150, 151, 154, 155, 157, 158, 164, 168, 174
perennial production with winter dormancy, 11
perennial vs. annual production, 8
perforated drying floor, 115
perlite, 38, 41, 45
pesticides, 3
pests and diseases, 86
pests,

in a greenhouse, 88
aphids, 88, 149
broad mites, 88, 89
mites, 88
rabbits, 88
scale, 88
thrips, 88
whiteflies, 88, 149
pH, 58, 61, 63, 150, 151, 158, 160, 164
phosphorous, 13, 24, 39, 42, 59, 61, 62, 64, 90, 92, 150, 158, 161, 162, 164, 171–173, 175, 176
phosphorus deficiency, 85
phosphorus solubilizing bacteria, 63
photoperiod, 15–17, 27, 28, 50
Pisa, Italy, 12, 25, 130, 164
plant hardiness zones, 7
plant light, 16, 40, 49, 137
plant spacing, 83, 97, 98, 128, 145, 150, 151, 157, 158, 166
planting, 7, 8, 17, 22, 25, 34, 47, 62, 65, 72, 75, 76, 78, 79, 83, 93–95, 96, 97, 101, 128–130, 142, 149, 154, 155, 157, 158, 160, 161, 163, 164, 166, 173, 176
planting densities,
  gross income comparisons, 96
  yield comparisons, 94, 96, 98, 99
  costs and benefits of a high planting density, 93
planting density, 47, 72, 74–76, 78, 80, 82, 83, 93–98, 101, 128, 130, 142, 145, 146, 151, 154, 155, 157, 158, 160, 161, 164, 166
plants, selling, 133
plastic, 9, 13, 23, 24, 40, 66, 69–80, 82, 93, 94, 98, 117, 121, 130, 139, 143, 160, 175–177

plastic bags for storing leaves, 121, 139
plastic mulch, 13, 65, 69–77, 79, 130, 148, 175–177
plowing, 60, 65, 142
plug production, 40, 88
plugs, 14, 100, 128, 134, 135, 142, 168, 171, 172
pollination of stevia, 5
Polyphagotarsonemus latus, 88
poor drainage, 57
potassium, 9, 13, 27, 47, 48, 59, 61, 62, 64, 85, 90–92, 146, 150, 158, 160–162, 164, 173
potassium deficiency, 85
potassium magnesia, 59, 162
potassium sulfate, 48, 146
pots, 41, 42, 45, 48–50, 54, 134, 135, 161, 171
potting soil, 38, 39, 45, 47, 48, 52, 54, 89, 134, 135, 173, 176, 177
powdered stevia leaf, 117, 167, 168
powdery mildew, 89
Prairie Oak Publishing, 128, 134, 135, 139, 170, 172
pre-conditioning mother plants, 49, 50
Premier Horticulture Inc., 177
prices for leaves, 129
pricing, 73, 74, 80, 82, 95, 96, 129, 132, 133
processing stevia leaves on-farm, 138
processors, 34, 123, 126, 127
production costs, 71, 76, 79, 83, 93, 127, 133, 134
production cycles, 7, 11, 25, 33, 53, 60, 68, 71, 73, 74, 79, 81–83, 93, 94, 96–99
propagating
  from stem cuttings, 44
  with crown divisions, 50, 53
propane heat, 115

pruning, 82–84, 166
pruning, yield increase, 83
PSB, 63
pythium, 89

R

rabbits, 88
rainfall, 7, 27, 68, 79, 137, 165
Rain-Flo Irrigation, LLC., 177
reaping hook, 106
Rebaudioside A, 1, 35, 59, 148, 161
reseeding, 5
retail sales, 43, 132
Rheinbach, Germany, 160
Rhizoctonia solani, 89, 92
Rhizoctonia solani Kuehn, 89
Richters Herbs, 35, 119, 121, 171, 178
ridge and furrow system, 66, 150
ridge tilling, 64
Robert Marvel Plastic Mulch, 176
rock phosphate, 64
root crowns, 4, 5, 13–15, 33–37, 51–54, 84, 90, 91, 137, 151, 158
root rot, 89, 90
roots, 5, 9, 13, 14, 26, 36, 44, 45, 47, 50–53, 55, 64, 68, 69, 78, 85, 88–92, 96, 135, 146, 151, 158, 161
rotary spading, 65
rotary tilling, 60, 65
Rottaia Agricultural Center, 165
row covers, 10, 22–24, 66, 78, 79, 128, 169, 173, 176, 177
rubbing screen, 116–118

S

S.J. Herbals and Health Care, 173
Sacramento Valley, 148
Sacramento, California, 12, 88, 147, 148
salads, 136

San Francisco Herb Co., 129, 178
San Piero a Grado, Italy, 164, 165
sand, 9, 48, 52, 61, 120, 146, 158, 160, 161
sandy clay loam, 39, 150
sandy loam soils, 58, 64, 72, 155, 160, 161
sandy soils, 39, 58, 62, 64, 69, 72, 142, 150, 155, 160, 161
scale (pest), 88
Schweiss Welding, 175
sclerotinia, 12, 91, 162
Sclerotinia sclerotiorum, 91
Sclerotium dephinii Welch, 91
Sclerotium rolfsii, 87, 90, 92
seed, 4, 5, 16, 33–43, 54, 76, 87, 88, 123, 124, 128, 130–132, 134, 135, 142, 149, 151, 158, 163, 164, 167, 168, 171–174, 176
seed germination, 5, 39, 40, 42
seed viability, 5, 8, 34, 131
seeders, automated, 41
seeders, hand, 41
seed-grown cultivars, 35
seedlings, 41, 42
Seedman.com, 173
selection as a breeding method, 54
septoria, 36, 87, 89–91, 143
septoria leaf spot, 36, 87, 89, 90
Septoria steviae, 90, 91, 143
Serres in Greece, 153
Seven Springs Farm, 177
shade cloth, 49
shading, 27
shipping of leaves, 104, 117, 121, 122
Shock, Clinton, 3, 48, 88, 147
shop light, 40, 45, 137
short-day, 15, 16, 27, 84
shredded leaf mulch, 70, 71
sickle, 106, 109
silt, 60, 61, 146, 158, 164
single-row system, 66, 109

Slovakia, 69, 74
slug, 12, 14, 88
smoothies, 136
soil, 3, 5, 14, 22, 36, 38, 39, 42, 49, 52, 57, 58, 60, 62, 63, 64, 66, 68–72, 75, 77, 79, 86, 87, 89, 91, 120, 124, 127, 128, 134, 142, 146, 149–151, 155, 158, 160, 161, 164, 177
soil fertility, 58, 64, 70
soil moisture, 68, 70
soil pH, 58, 61, 63, 150, 151, 158, 160, 164
soil structure, 64
South Bengal, India, 90
southern blight, 92
Southern Crop Protection and Food Research Centre, 109, 119, 143, 144
southern hemisphere, 21
spring, 9, 10, 12–15, 18, 20, 21, 23, 26, 49, 51, 55, 78, 88, 146, 151, 162
St. Augustine, Florida, 11
standing water, 57, 64, 68
Starwest Botanicals, Inc., 178
stem cuttings, 4, 33–36, 39, 44–49, 51, 88, 89, 135, 146, 155, 157, 160, 161, 163, 171, 172
stem rot, 89, 91
stem tips, 47, 48, 68, 82, 83, 116, 137, 146, 157, 166
stevia extract powder, 35, 138, 170
stevia extracts, 126, 167
stevioside, 16, 24, 34, 35, 58, 65, 104, 110–112, 117, 137, 163
stevioside extract, 126, 167
stevioside yield, 35
Steviva Brands, Inc., 168
storage of leaves, 104, 112, 121, 128, 139, 143, 149
strapping for boxes, 122
straw mulch, 9, 14, 52, 70, 71, 75, 76, 77, 78, 149

subtropical climate, 4
sugar, 1, 2, 3, 13, 58, 139, 153, 166, 168, 170
sugar cane, 2
Sukabumi, West Java, Indonesia, 72–74, 99, 155
sulfur deficiency, 85
summer, 5, 17, 19, 21, 25, 26, 51, 57, 71, 77, 80, 93, 145, 146, 148–150, 153, 158, 160, 163, 164, 166
Sun Fruits Ltd., 168, 174
Sun Gro Horticulture, Inc., 177
Sunfruits Ltd., 67, 100
sunlight, 7, 16, 111
sunshine and glycoside content, 16
superphosphate, 48, 146

T

Tamil Nadu State of India, 90
Tasmania, 12
tea cut leaf, 103, 116–118, 123
tea herbs, 124, 136, 137
temperature, 4, 7–9, 11–14, 17, 21–27, 40, 42, 43, 47, 49, 52, 70, 71, 74, 77, 79, 90, 105, 110, 115, 116, 131, 155
tender perennial, 4, 8
tensiometer, 68
Texas, 11
The Grower's Exchange, 171
thrips, 88
Tifton, Georgia, 11
tillering, 5
tip pruning, 82–84
tissue culture, 33, 34, 36, 37, 54, 158
Tithorea in Greece, 153
tobacco, 3, 91, 131, 143, 153
Tomato Spotted Wilt Virus, 89, 91
Toumpa in Greece, 153
trace minerals, 64
tractor, 65, 71, 78, 95, 97, 101, 106, 108, 109, 143

transplant timing
  above 15° latitude, 21
  below 15° latitude, 27
transplanter, 40, 71, 97, 101, 172, 175–177
transplanting, 18, 20–24, 27, 37, 43, 48, 53, 61, 63, 69, 71, 76, 83, 100, 101, 128, 150, 151, 165, 166
transplanting to the field, 100
transplanting, labor requirement, 101
transplants, 39, 40, 88, 94, 100, 124, 128, 142, 146, 149, 151, 155, 157, 158, 161, 164
transport wagon, 115
tropical climate, 11, 62, 63, 72, 77, 96, 150, 154, 155, 157, 168
tropical monsoon climate, 63

U

United States, 2, 7, 8, 11, 23, 25, 27, 66, 68, 73, 77, 80, 82, 88, 91, 95, 96, 119, 129, 131–133, 135, 138, 145, 146, 148, 149, 152, 171, 172, 177
University of Bonn, 48, 162
University of Thessaly, 3, 153
urea, 48, 61, 62, 142, 146, 155, 159
US Department of Agriculture, 2, 3, 7–9, 11–13, 21, 23, 68, 86, 88, 138, 145, 146, 148, 149
USDA, 2, 3, 7–9, 11–13, 21, 23, 68, 86, 88, 138, 145, 146, 148, 149
USDA Plant Hardiness Zones, 7–9, 11–13, 23, 68, 145, 146, 148, 149
Uttar Pradesh, India, 13

V

VAM, 63
Vanashree Agrotech, 173

vermiculite, 38, 41, 45
Vermont Compost Company, 177
Verticillium dahliae, 89, 91
vesicular arbuscular mycorrhiza, 63
Victorville, California, 11

W

Washington State University, 71
water supply, 69
weed control, 28, 65, 70, 71, 75–78, 127, 128, 143, 148, 152, 155, 159, 176
weeding, cost, 78
white plastic mulch, 74
white stevia extract powder, 35, 138, 170
whiteflies, 88, 149
wholesale, 34, 103, 117, 125, 127, 129, 132–135, 139, 171, 172
Wichita, Kansas, 68, 145
wild plants, 5
Wind Hill Native Gardens, 171
winnowing and screening leaves, 120
winter, 8–14, 19, 21, 25, 26, 48–51, 55, 88, 130, 146, 148, 151, 161, 164
winter dormancy, 9, 11, 13, 25, 88, 130, 146, 148, 151, 164
winter survival, 9, 10
wintered-over plants, 49

X

Xanthi in Greece, 153

Y

yield, stevia, 2, 3, 5, 7, 9, 15, 16, 22, 24–26, 28, 33, 35, 36–38, 47, 49, 53, 54, 58, 60–66, 71–75, 77, 79–83, 93–96, 98, 104,

105, 126–131, 137, 141, 142, 145–152, 155, 157–166
yield summaries,
   large-scale, 131
   small-scale trials, 130

Z

Zagliveri in Greece, 153
zinc toxicity, 86

About the Author

Jeffrey Goettemoeller grew up gardening alongside his dad and went on to earn a B.S. degree with a major in horticulture at Northwest Missouri State University. Under the direction of Dr. Alejandro Ching, Jeffrey also completed a published research study on the production of Stevia rebaudiana seeds. Years later, he still grows and studies stevia. Jeffrey is the author of *Stevia Sweet Recipes: Sugar-free—Naturally!*, with over 300,000 copies in print, and *Growing and Using Stevia: The Sweet Leaf from Garden to Table with 35 Recipes*.

www.prairieoakpublishing.com
www.growingstevia.com

More Books from Prairie Oak Publishing

Growing and Using Stevia: The Sweet Leaf from Garden to Table with 35 Recipes. Authors Jeffrey Goettemoeller and Karen Lucke. 2008. ISBN 978-0-9786293-3-5. Available in English, German, Polish, and Spanish language editions.

Sustainable Ethanol: Biofuels, Biorefineries, Cellulosic Biomass, Flex-Fuel Vehicles, and Sustainable Farming for Energy Independence. Authors Jeffrey Goettemoeller and Adrian Goettemoeller. ISBN 978-0-9786293-0-4.